Advent and Lenten Lectionary Workbook

Fiscal Year 1991

C.S.S. Publishing Co., Inc.

Lima, Ohio

Copyright © 1990 by
The C.S.S. Publishing Company, Inc.
Lima, Ohio

Library of Congress Cataloging-in-Publication Data
(Revised for vol. 2)

Bass, George M., 1920-
    Lectionary preaching workbook, series III.

    Contents: [v. 1] Cycle A — [v. 2] Cycle B.
    1. Preaching. 2. Bible—Liturgical lessons, English. 3. Bible—Homiletical use. 4. Sermons—Outlines, syllabi, etc. 5. Church year—Prayer books and devotions—English. 6. Common lectionary. I. Title
BV4211.2.B267   1989   251   89-9971
ISBN 1-55673-135-3 (v. 1)
ISBN 1-55673-252-X (v. 2 — 8½ x 11 size)
ISBN 1-55673-243-0 (v. 2 — 5½ x 8½ size)
ISBN 1-55673-297-x (v. 2 — 8½ x 11 size - U.W. Armed Forces Version)

Introduction

Four decades ago, Andrew W. Blackwood taught a preaching course at Temple University that he titled after a book, *Planning a Year's Pulpit Work.* That course was this writer's first exposure to the subject of planning one's sermons on a long-term basis. Blackwood's thesis was that good preaching involves what H. Grady Davis a decade later would call a "germinal period:" That is, good sermons need time to germinate and develop. Blackwood believed, therefore, that every preacher should have a "homiletical seedplot" — a long-term plan by which he/she might work as much as a year ahead in the planning and development of sermons. Rarely, he believed, could an excellent sermon be put together in a couple of days, let alone overnight. The preaching process needs to be organized and systematic to assure that preachers will do their best when they step into the pulpit to preach each Sunday.

This preacher saw the wisdom in Blackwood's thesis, but did little about adapting his plan to preaching from a lectionary. One type of preaching that Andrew Blackwood suggested was the Reformed pattern of preaching through books of the Bible in the manner of John Calvin in Geneva. He suggested preaching on four books of scripture every year as part of a multi-year plan that one might institute on assuming a new pastorate. His rationale was similar to that of the Roman Catholic Church insistence (in the *Constitution of the Sacred Liturgy* of Vatican II) that people do not know the scriptures and that, accordingly, more of the Bible has to be read and preached in Sunday worship services. Blackwood concluded that teaching the Bible is an important part of any homiletical regimen, emphasizing the role of expository preaching in pulpit ministry in his book on the development of expository sermons. Expository preaching became (under Blackwood and the impact of other homileticians and biblical scholars) the homiletical order of the day. But few people adopted the long-term plan suggested by Andrew Blackwood for parish preaching.

In my own case, it was a couple of years after taking Blackwood's course — and after moving to my second parish — that I adapted his approach of planning my preaching program around lectionary preaching. While in Harrisburg, Pennsylvania, I became acquainted with Rev. C. Arthur Neal, Jr., a young pastor who had developed a reputation for excellent parish preaching. He revealed his secret to me in conversation: he planned his year's preaching during his summer vacation. By the beginning of September each year, he had a clear idea of the shape and themes of his preaching ministry for the coming year. He has served his congregation in Camp Hill, Pennsylvania, for over thirty-five years, and his parish has continued to grow. I suspect that his preaching has had much to do with his longevity and his continued effectiveness as a parish — and preaching — pastor. My guess is that he continues to plan his preaching for the next year every summer. It was his influence and that of Andrew Blackwood that caused me to begin long-term planning of my preaching ministry.

It was my study of Martin Luther's *Church Postils,* begun during this brief pastorate, that helped me to make the transition from Blackwood's "Bible-book" program of more or less didactic preaching to a plan that accommodates liturgy, lectionary, and the church year. *Church Postils* were sermons prepared in 1520 at the request of the Elector Frederick to supply the clergy, many of whom were incapable of preparing effective sermons, with models for study or even for reading in the pulpit on Sundays. Accordingly, the first postils (*post illa verba* — "after the word") were written when Luther was in hiding in Wartburg. They appeared in 1521 in Latin, and were translated into German. His first postils were on the Gospels; the second series on the Epistles. One source insists that all of the gospel postils were written at Wartburg and the epistle sermons were written the next year, while another authority claims that the *Church Postils* took from 1520-1527 to reach publication. They went through several editions during his lifetime, and since his death a new edition has been published.

Luther wrote the postils himself during the only period of his ministry when he actually wrote out his sermons. In the process, he preserved the lectionary, emphasized the importance of sermon preparation, and laid the foundation for the planning of lectionary sermons on a long-term basis.

Modern scientific study of the scriptures supports the importance of long-term sermon planning that involves careful study of the lections as integral to homiletical production and effectiveness. The preacher who intends to preach on the Gospel for the Day needs to discern the different reasons that the Evangelists wrote their Gospels, and the variations in situation, intention, and theological emphases in the Gospels. The logical procedure, in this regard, is to make a study of the Gospel of the Year before one begins to preach in Advent of any given year. This amounts to the first step in "planning a year's pulpit work." A reading of the complete Gospel of the Year is part of this procedure, of course. The second step is to read each of the pericopes for every Sunday of the year to comprehend the relationship of the lessons to each other, the Sunday, the season, and the cycle of the church year. A study of each part of the propers for any Sunday, with concentrated work on the preaching text, opens the way for developing the individual subjects, topics, themes, and tentative titles for forthcoming sermons. Fred Craddock calls this "listening" to the word a crucial step in sermon preparation.

A helpful tool for developing sermons within a long-range plan is a "Sermon Planner/Builder" worksheet for each sermon to be preached during the year. The following "planner/builder" is one that I have used and have found to be indispensable in planning sermons. I have used a similar one to write sermons for publication, as well. This "planner/builder" will not fit every preacher's needs or methods, but each pastor should construct a similar vehicle to employ while planning his/her preaching ministry. A series of sermon files — or the adaptation of this procedure to a computer/word processor filing system — will facilitate your sermon planning/building.

The Components of Cycle B Preaching

The Lectionary, Liturgy, and Church Year in Perspective

The lectionary is the servant of the liturgy and the worship of the Church; it does not exist solely for the sake of preaching. Christians gather together on Sundays to hear the "Good Word" and to celebrate the death, resurrection, and anticipated return of Jesus Christ to the world at the end of time. (I call this the Tree, the Tomb, and the Trumpet — the very heart of the Gospel of our Lord.) The lectionary supports worship by focusing the liturgy upon these saving events, rearranging the story so that it is told and retold, Sunday after Sunday, in the reading and preaching of the Word and the celebration of the sacraments. The lectionary serves the liturgy of the church by articulating the Gospel during the cycles, seasons, and Sundays of the church year. It is a serious error to perceive the lectionary solely as a tool for preaching the Word to God's people.

The liturgy is the response of the people of God to his grace in Christ Jesus. It is the song they sing; their reply to the story of his saving action in Jesus. The church year "beats time," establishing the rhythm for the singing of this song, as well as the preaching of the Gospel, by reminding the church that each Sunday is a "little Easter" — a celebration of Jesus' resurrection and of the hope people have in the risen Lord. This is the context in which Christian pastors preach the Word to their people. Preaching has to be related to the worship and liturgy of the church if it is to uncover the heart of the Gospel — Jesus' death and resurrection — and spell out the wonders of God's love and grace to people who are hurting and longing for a word of assurance, peace, and hope.

The church year also spreads out the redeeming events of the Gospel over the entire course of the year, making the first half of the year — the Christmas and Easter cycles — a time when the heart of the Gospel is articulated in worship and preaching, and completing the rest of the story in the Pentecost cycle/season so that the essential parts of the Gospel will be read and preached in the liturgy of the church. The three-year lectionary follows its direction and gives the different versions of the four Evangelists in the appropriate cycles, seasons, and Sundays of any given year. It is the church year that sets the Gospel content for specific Sundays, thereby rearranging the gospel story in the liturgy of the Church. *Thus, the church year is the key to the planning of one's preaching and worship for the year. It offers to the parish preacher a ready-made plan for planning and building sermons.*

Year B — The Gospels of St. Mark and St. John

The second year of the three-year lectionary really ought to be called the Year of St. Mark *and* St. John, not simply the year of Mark. Thirty of the Gospels appointed for the Sundays of the year are from the Gospel of St. Mark; twenty are from the Gospel of St. John. (The other two are from Matthew and Luke.) In the Christmas cycle, Mark is read six times, while John is assigned to four Sundays. There are four selections from Mark in the Easter cycle, eight from John and one from Luke. Mark will be read on twenty Sundays in Pentecost in 1992; John on eight occasions. Thus, Mark and John have almost equal liturgical/homiletical billing during Advent, Christmas, and Epiphany, while John shares Lent with Mark but dominates Holy Week and the Easter Gospels. Mark comes into its own during the Pentecost cycle/season. *One has to conclude that Year B is the Year of St. John as well as of St. Mark.*

Those pastors who preach on the Gospels in Year B will be preaching from two radically different perspectives. (This is true in Years A and C, too, when John is again assigned to portions of the year, but not to the same extent as in Year B.) If one has recognized this and has done some detailed study in conjunction with John's Gospel for Year A, one's preliminary work is somewhat simplified. If not, background reading must be done on both Mark and John before beginning to work on specific texts for the planning and development of sermons. One preaches the Gospel in Year B from two different perspectives — that of Mark and that of John — and they *are* different. Each needs to be examined in some detail.

The Gospel of St. Mark for preachers

Virtually all New Testament scholars agree that Mark was the first Gospel to be set down in written form. This means that Mark undertook the task of creating a type of literature that would be faithful to the church's oral witness to the Gospel of the Lord. *The heart of Mark's Gospel is that the Lord is alive. He has conquered sin and death and will return, as he said, in God's good time.* That could be why over one-third of Mark's version of the Gospel is devoted to the last week Jesus spent in Jerusalem. It was probably written shortly after Nero's terrible persecutions of the Christians that had taken place in Rome. Where it was composed is a matter of speculation. Some scholars still claim that Rome was the locus for Mark, while others have suggested that Mark could have been written in Antioch, or even in Galilee or Syria.

Mark as proclamation

Mark is "shot full of holes" by apparent errors and mistakes — sequence of events, time gaps, literary mistakes, incorrect names and places — and cannot be considered to be an attempt at setting down the history or complete biography of Jesus Christ. It is simply too brief and, from one point of view, sketchy. What it does do, however, is arrange the story of Jesus in such a manner to make a theological point: Jesus, Mark makes clear right from the start of his Gospel, is the *Christ*, the promised one of God. But Mark also reports that Jesus called himself the *Son of Man* — a title used in conjunction with his earthly ministry, his suffering and death, as well as his return at the end of the age. *Mark tells the story of Jesus, the Son of Man, who is the Promised One of God who has brought the Kingdom of God into reality in the world. Mark's Gospel is a story, not simply the history of Jesus Christ. This Jesus will bring in the fullness of the Kingdom on his return to earth.*

The Gospel of Mark is cast in a new literary form so that the Good News will be proclaimed to the listeners. Mark sought to correct christological errors and to emphasize the central theological truth of the Gospel — Jesus' death, resurrection, and the parousia — and to do this he simply wrote down the story from his point of view in light of the theological situation of the church. It is also obvious that story was the best vehicle he could employ to allow the living Lord to speak to, and to instruct, his people. There can be no doubt that Mark wrote for a believing audience whose faith needed to be undergirded christologically and theologically. He recognized that they needed to hear Jesus' words to live as faithful followers of the risen Lord. His interest was ethical, not simply moral.

Dietrich Bonhoeffer agrees: *The Christian life is the life of Christ. . . . Christian life is the dawning of the ultimate in me; it is the life of Jesus Christ in me. . . . Christian life means being a man through the efficacy of the incarnation; it means being sentenced and pardoned through the efficacy of the cross; and it means living a new life through the efficacy of the resurrection. There cannot be one of these without the rest. (Ethics, p. 122)*

Mark and the lectionary

Archbishop William Carrington, a New Testament scholar, several decades ago advanced the theory that Mark was not only written in Rome (the "Gospel of Rome"), but that Mark's structure suggests that it also fit into the primitive church year (Easter and the Pasch and the Great Fifty Days) quite well. He concluded that it was in the shape of a primitive lectionary, read and proclaimed at Sunday worship during the developmental period of church year and lectionary. His theory is interesting, and a few scholars think there is some merit to it, although most reject his thesis on the basis of more recent scholarship. However, it does have some ramifications for the modern three-year lectionary and the revised church year.

One could argue that Mark should have been the Gospel for Year/Cycle A rather than for Year/Cycle B; not because it is the first Gospel, chronologically, but because its focus is on the very heart of the Gospel — the redeeming event we know as the resurrection of Jesus Christ (what I have previously called the Tree, Tomb, and the Trumpet). The death of Jesus, his victory over death and the grave, and the expectation of his return are all part of the resurrection — both in Mark and in the church year, as well. *The resurrection of Jesus is the heart of the Gospel, the nucleus of the church year, and central event in the lectionary of the Christian church.*

Various scholars contend that chapter 13 is the key chapter of Mark, proclaiming the return and ultimate victory of the risen and living Christ to the earth. Mark 13:33-37, which exhorts the faithful to watch for the coming of the Lord, is the Gospel for the First Sunday in Advent. As part of the proclamation of the resurrection, the parousia is announced to prepare the church for the final chapter of the sacred story of Jesus Christ. This lection alone, in the context of the entire chapter, is the very heart of Mark's Gospel and suggests that Mark might have been the Gospel for Year/Cycle A rather than for B. The Gospels of Matthew and Luke (assigned to Advent 1) articulate a similar, even identical theme, but the very nature of Mark's Gospel more forcefully makes the point.

Preaching the Gospel of Mark calls for pastors to keep Mark's eschatological perspective in mind *as the central theme of Mark's Gospel,* and to allow this promised event to bring all of the other details of Mark's story into kerygmatic focus. *The cross, resurrection, and parousia are inextricably connected to each other, according to Mark, and should inform — implicitly and/or explicitly — every sermon preached.* Preaching from the lectionary and the church year is preaching from the kerygmatic perspective of St. Mark.

The Gospel of John for preachers

John is rather obviously different from the other — synoptic — Gospels. This is so because he paints a *different picture of Jesus* than do Mark, Matthew, and Luke. John's Jesus doesn't speak in parables, but gives long, rather abstract speeches. He only performs seven miracles, and these are the basis for the controversy and discussion. He doesn't cure masses of people, as does the Jesus of the other Gospels. This Jesus speaks about the life he knew with God before his incarnation. John turns around the key statement of the risen Lord about the parousia and, puts it at the beginning of his Gospel. Jesus has come from the Father to reveal himself through signs, miracles, and his teaching, and to suffer and die — and rise again — in order to complete his appointed mission on earth. Those who hear John's story of Jesus have to decide whether they believe it — they must choose between light and life, darkness and death.

Jesus, according to John, comes to earth bearing gifts from heaven itself. These gifts are in his person, and so he gives earthly, this-worldly names to him — bread, water, light, life. He demonstrates his Lordship over life by working miracles: feeding, providing water, and even by raising Lazarus from the dead to reveal God's glory gift — a life that cannot be conquered by death. Truly, Jesus is "the resurrection and the life," now and in the Gospel of John. The resurrected life is a gift of grace from God — in baptism — through Jesus. Jesus was concerned with giving lasting, eternal gifts to people, not with improving our life-style and longevity here on earth.

John confronts people with his interpretation of the Gospel so that they might believe. He is concerned about people's faith — our faith — and declares: "These things have been written so that you may believe that Jesus is the Messiah, the Son of God, and believing have life in his name." To unbelievers, Jesus makes seemingly preposterous claims in his speeches and teachings to the people: "I am the bread of life," "Destroy this temple, and in three days I will raise it up," or "My kingship is not of this world . . . . You say that I am a king. For this I was born and for this I came into the world, to bear witness to the truth. Every one who is of the truth hears my voice." There is a challenge to believe in every word he utters. Those who hear this Gospel are confronted with the crisis of deciding between judgment and death, or faith, forgiveness, and life.

Raymond Brown offers some suggestions for preachers in his article, "The Johannine World for Preachers" (*Interpretation,* vol. 43, no. 1, January 1989).

1. "Do not be afraid to use ingenuity in rendering this dramatic Gospel dramatically." He suggests "staging" the stories by involving people in a type of chancel drama, or in preaching the sermon *before* the Gospel is read.

2. "Do not domesticate the Johannine Jesus." Wrestle with, do not avoid, difficult verses and passages which sound quite offensive and puzzling. ". . . But do not silence this Jesus by deciding what he should not have said and what your hearers should not hear."

3. "Do not be too sophisticated or abstract in preaching the Jesus of John." Jesus, says Brown, "is not the founder of Christianity who lived 'way back then.' *He is alive and well, giving life to every branch on the vine, calling his sheep by name and expecting them to recognize his voice. He knows those who believe in him and he loves them; and he expects love in return, not faith alone."* [Emphasis mine.] Raymond Brown believes that "the sophisticated preacher who has written off 'Jesus loves me' as appropriate only to another style of Christianity is not going to do justice to John." That Jesus has love for all people must be reflected in the concern and care of faithful Christians for others, if it is to be valid in the eyes of the living Lord.

Preaching Resources for Series B

Commentaries on the Gospel of Mark
Achtemeier, Paul, *Mark (Proclamation Commentaries),* Fortress, 1975.
Juel, Donald, *Mark* (Augsburg Series), Fortress, 1990.
Kee, Howard Clark, *The Community of the New Age,* Fortress, 1974.
Kelber, Werner, *The Kingdom in Mark,* Fortress, 1974.
Kelber, Werner, *Mark's Story of Jesus,* Fortress.
Rhoads, Daniel and David Michie, *Mark as Story,* Fortress, 1982.
Robbins, Vernon K., *Jesus the Teacher,* Fortress, 1974.
Weden, Theodore, *Mark: Traditions in Conflict, Fortress, 1971.*

Other Commentaries
Achtemeier, Elizabeth, *The Old Testament and the Proclamation of the Gospel,* Westminster, 1982.
Brown, Raymond E., *The Gospel of John* (volumes 1 and 2), Doubleday.
Craddock, Hayes and Holloday, *Preaching the New Common Lectionary,* Abingdon, 1984.
Fuller, Reginald, *Preaching the New Lectionary,* The Liturgical Press, 1974.
McCurley, Foster, *Proclaiming the Promise,* Fortress, 1975.
Proclamation (various volumes), Fortress, 1973-present.
Sloyan, Gerard, *A Commentary on the New Lectionary,* Paulist Press, 1975.

Church Year
Board of Discipleship, United Methodist Church, *Seasons of the Gospel,* Abingdon.
Gibson, George A., *The Story of the Church Year.*
Nocent, Adrian, *The Liturgical Year* (Four volumes), The Liturgical Press, 1977.
Rochelle, Jay, *The Revolutionary Year,* Fortress, 1971.

Other Church Year Preaching Aids
Augsburg Sermons (annual)
Concordia Pulpit (annual)
C.S.S. (Lectionary Sermon Sets)
Emphasis, C.S.S.
Homily Service, Liturgical Conference, Washington, D.C.
Lectionary Homiletics (monthly), David B. Howell, ed., Midlothian, VA
The Minister's Annual Manual (for preaching and worship planning), Lois and Manfred Holck, ed., Austin, TX.
Preaching Helps (published formerly by Seminex)

Liturgical Preaching
Babin, David, *Week In — Week Out,* Seabury, 1976.
Bass, George M., *The Renewal of Liturgical Preaching,* Augsburg, 1967.
Bosch, Paul, *The Sermon as Part of the Liturgy,* Concordia, 1977.
Fuller, Reginald, *What is Liturgical Preaching?,* SCM Press, 1957.
Lischer, Richard, *A Theology of Preaching,* Abingdon, 1971.
Skudlarek, William, *The Word in Worship: Preaching in a Liturgical Context,* Abingdon, 1981.
Willimon, William H., *Preaching and Worship,* Westminster, 1984.

Contemporary Homiletics

Achtemeier, Elizabeth, *Creative Preaching: Finding the Words,* Abingdon, 1980.

Achtemeier, Elizabeth, *Preaching as Theology and Art,* Abingdon, 1984.

Bass, George M., *The Song and the Story,* C.S.S., 1984.

Buechner, Frederick, *Telling the Truth: The Gospel as Tragedy, Comedy, and Fairy Tale,* Harper and Row, 1977.

Burghardt, Walter, *Preaching: The Art and Craft,* Paulist Press, 1987.

Buttrick, David, *Homiletic: Moves and Structures,* Fortress, 1987.

Buttrick, David, *A Theology of Preaching,* Fortress, 1988.

Carl, William J., *Preaching Christian Doctrine,* Fortress, 1984.

Cox, James W., ed., *Biblical Preaching: An Expositor's Treasury,* Westminster, 1983.

Craddock, Fred B., *Preaching,* Abingdon, 1985.

Craddock, Fred B., *As One Without Authority,* Abingdon, 1979.

Craddock, Fred B., *Overhearing the Gospel,* Abingdon, 1978.

Crum, Milton, *Manual on Preaching,* Judson, 1977.

Ellingsen, Mark C., *Doctrine and Word,* Westminster, 1983.

Ellingsen, Mark C., *The Integrity of Biblical Narratives*, Augsburg Fortress, 1990.

Erdahl, Lowell, *Preaching for the People,* Harper and Row, 1978.

Fant, Clyde E., *Preaching for Today,* Harper and Row, 1987 (revised).

Fuller, Reginald, *The Use of the Bible in Preaching,* Fortress, 1981.

Halvorson, Arndt, *Authentic Preaching,* Augsburg, 1982.

Jensen, Richard, *Telling the Story,* Augsburg, 1980.

Keck, Leander E., *The Bible in the Pulpit,* Abingdon, 1978.

Killinger, John, *Fundamentals of Preaching,* Fortress, 1986.

Long, Thomas, *Preaching and the Literary Forms of the Bible,* Fortress, 1989.

Long, Thomas, *The Senses of Preaching,* John Knox, 1988.

Lowry, Eugene, *Doing Time in the Pulpit,* Abingdon, 1985.

Lowry, Eugene, *The Homiletic Plot,* John Knox, 1983.

Marquart, Edward F., *Quest for Better Preaching,* Augsburg, 1985.

Mitchell, Henry M., *The Recovery of Preaching,* Harper and Row, 1977.

Nichols, J. Randall, *Building the Word: The Dynamics of Communication and Preaching,* Harper and Row, 1981.

O'Day, Gail R., *The Word Disclosed: John's Story and Narrative Preaching,* CBP Press, 1987.

Patte, Daniel, *Preaching Paul,* Fortress, 1984.

Rice, Charles A., *Interpretation and Imagination,* Fortress, 1970 (reprinted, 1987)

Salmon, Bruce C., *Storytelling in Preaching,* Broadman Press, 1988.

Sanders, James A., *God Has a Story Too: Biblical Sermons in Context,* Fortress, 1979.

Sleeth, Ronald E., *God's Words and Our Words,* John Knox, 1986.

Smith, J. Alfred, *Preach On!*, Broadman, 1984.

Steimle, E. A., M. Neidenthal, and C. Rice., *Preaching the Story,* Fortress, 1980.

Stott, John R., *Between Two Worlds: The Art of Preaching in the Twentieth Century,* Eerdmann's, 1982.

Thompson, William, *Exegesis and Interpretation,* Abingdon, 1981.

Thulin, Richard, *The "I" in the Story,* Augsburg Fortress, 1989.

Tostengard, Sheldon, *The Spoken Word,* Augsburg Fortress, 1989.

Tribble, Phyllis, *God and the Rhetoric of Sexuality,* Fortress, 1978.

Wardlaw, Don E., *Preaching Biblically: Creating Sermons in the Shape of Scripture,* Westminster, 1983.

Williams, Michael E., *Preaching Peers,* Discipleship Resources, 1987.

Williams, Michael E., *Preaching Pilgrims,* Discipleship Resources, 1988.

Wilson, Paul Scott, *Imaginations of the Heart: New Understandings in Preaching,* Abingdon, 1988.

(Note: For an exhaustive bibliography on preaching and contemporary homiletics, see David Buttrick's *homiletic.*)

The Christmas Cycle

The Christmas Cycle is composed of three integrated seasons: Advent, Christmas, and Epiphany. It might better be called the Advent, or the Parousia, Cycle, because it centers on the return, the Second Coming, of Christ in judgment rather than, as popularly believed — and even suggested by the title of the cycle — on the birth of Jesus as the First Coming of our Lord. It establishes an *eschatological* perspective for the entire Christian year, not only in the season of Advent, but in Christmas and Epiphany, as well, reminding the faithful that the full plan of God's redemption of the world will not be initiated until the time comes that God has determined for Jesus' return in glory. The cycle varies, in most years, from twelve to fourteen weeks in length (in 1990-91, it will be eleven weeks long), so that it is approximately one quarter of the calendar. This is important for planning one's preaching ministry; the very nature of the season seems to suggest that coherence and unity in the reading of the Gospel (and supporting lessons) might best be achieved if "inclusive planning" — for all three of the seasons — is done before one begins to preach on any of the Sundays of Advent.

Advent, consisting of the four Sundays immediately preceding Christmas, emphasizes the presence of the Lord in the proclamation of the Word and, especially, in the celebration of the Eucharist. The Sundays have the same basic content in all three series of Gospels, Matthew (A), Mark and John (B), and Luke (C):

1st Sunday in Advent ("Wake up" Sunday) — "Christ will come again!";

2nd Sunday in Advent (Preparation Sunday) — "The way of the Lord has been prepared";

3rd Sunday in Advent (Presence Sunday) — "The Lord, who will return, is even present now";

4th Sunday in Advent (Promise Sunday) — "God has kept his promise to send a Savior for all people." *("He will come again, as he said.")*

Advent, therefore, is oriented, as these themes recur and are expanded in the Gospels and the other lessons assigned annually to the Sundays of Advent, to the three "comings" of Christ. *Advent does not exist primarily to prepare the church for the celebration of Christmas; it has an ultimate purpose — to prepare the people of God for the Parousia.* Advent was probably evolved as a kind of "winter Lent" that was connected to Epiphany, a baptismal festival in the early Church (see my book *The Renewal of Liturgical Preaching* for additional information about the relationship of Advent to Epiphany. Adrian Nocent, in *The Liturgical Year,* treats the liturgical development of Advent in significant detail, revealing that, compared to Advent, Christmas was a "liturgical latecomer.") Advent, as an eschatological season, establishes the liturgical perspective for the entire year — the crucified, risen, and ascended Lord will come again! The Easter Christ himself has made this promise to his people.

Liturgical colors for Advent: blue or violet.

Christmas, despite the fact that it is popularly observed as a one-day festival (I call it a *one day wonder*), is a twelve-day season that finds popular — and almost singular — expression in the familiar carol, "The Twelve Days of Christmas." (Christmas Day — the "remnant" of the Christmas season — falls on a Tuesday in 1990.) Twelfth Night, the eve of Epiphany, which really concludes the Christmas season, is given some expression in the controlled burning of Christmas trees and, rather rarely of late, in the worship plans and patterns of some congregations. (Epiphany, unless it occurs on a Sunday, tends to be omitted from worship plans and sacramental practices, as well as popular piety. The Church has nearly forgotten that Epiphany was a reserve day for baptisms in the earlier history of the Church.) The other problem, which is equally serious for the worship life and spiritual growth of the faithful, is the reality that *Christmas is popularly celebrated during Advent; the Christmas festival is — really — the end of the Advent season rather than the beginning of a twelve-day celebration* of the birth of Jesus that finds ultimate expression in his death and resurrection and the promise of his coming to the world a second time. *Christmas — in the Christ Mass — finds eschatological orientation* in the Holy Communion, which always is a celebration of the *presence* of the risen Lord *and* the Parousia: "as often as you eat this bread and drink the cup, you proclaim the Lord's death until he comes (again)." (1 Corinthians 11:26) Thematically, the proclamation of the Gospel needs the twelve-day Christmas season to reestablish annually the full meaning of Christmas in the life of the church. Liturgically- and lectionary-oriented preaching *during Advent and Christmas* can go a long way in achieving this.

Liturgical colors for Christmas: white or gold.

Epiphany is, in many respects, a season that is "up for grabs." While the churches agree on how the Gospel should be read in all three years — semi-continuously, beginning with the Epiphany account of Jesus' birth (Matthew 2:1-13) — they don't agree on the naming of the Sundays after Epiphany. The Roman *Ordo* of the post-Vatican II liturgical reforms names the Sundays after Epiphany as Sundays "in Ordinary Time;" the Sundays after Pentecost were given the same "Ordinary Time" designation. Episcopalians, Lutherans, and others decided to call the same Sundays "after Epiphany" (the First Sunday after the Epiphany is celebrated as the "Baptism of Our Lord") and "after Pentecost." (The Episcopal lectionary and the Common lectionary count the Sundays after Pentecost by "Propers" — Proper 1, Proper 2, and so forth.) When seen the latter way, and despite the fact that the same Gospels and most of the other lessons are assigned to these Sundays by Roman Catholics and non-Romans, the Lutheran arrangement has more eschatological content — *realized eschatology* — stressing Jesus' manifestation to the world at his birth, his Baptism, ministry, and at his Transfiguration. Lutherans in the United States have celebrated the Transfiguration on the last Sunday after the Epiphany, partly as an echo of God's announcement at Jesus' Baptism ("you are my Son"), and also to serve as a climax to the Epiphany season and a bridge into the Easter Cycle (Lent and Easter seasons). The Gospels of Epiphany amplify the announcement of the Coming of the Christ to the world that was made at Jesus' birth. This remains the *manifestation* of the Messiah to Israel and, then, to the Gentile world, as well, and it completes the Christmas Cycle.

Liturgical colors for Epiphany: white (Epiphany, The Baptism of our Lord, and the Transfiguration) and green for the other Sundays.

Preaching in the Advent Season
Preaching the Advent themes is not easy, simply because it is eschatological preaching and such preaching is always difficult. Some preachers dodge the eschatological note on the First Sunday in Advent, the Second Coming of the Christ, by preaching on the "new church year." A quasi-liturgical "new year's sermon," which has no foundation in the lections for the day and is, therefore, topical, is the result. The context for preaching the Parousia during Advent is always *eschatological* — the birth, life, ministry, death, resurrection, and ascension of the Lord. When one's Advent sermons are oriented primarily toward the historical birth of Christ, rather than toward the fuller theological meaning of the *incarnation which has already taken place*, the theological orientation of the entire church year is in jeopardy. *Christ doesn't come at Christmas any differently than he comes to us at any other time of the year; he comes in the word and the sacraments of Baptism and the Eucharist. Every eucharistic celebration has the quality of future eschatology, because Christ is not only present in the meal through the Holy Spirit, but God's promise is proclaimed and renewed that the risen, ascended Lord will come again.*

Advent, it should be reiterated, establishes the kerygmatic perspective for Christian preaching for the entire year by sounding the note of future eschatology — Christ will come again! This, of course, complicates the preaching task of the pastor, demanding that pastoral preaching and teaching be done within this theological agenda. (What does all of this "second-coming business" have to do with me and my life here and now?) Christians are in the same predicament that Israel was in as they awaited the coming of the Messiah; nearly 2,000 years have passed and he has not returned as he said he would. Will he come again? Can he keep his promise to the church? Is it possible for the Lord to return in glory to judge the world at the end of the age? These are more likely to be the questions asked by contemporary Christians rather than *"when* will he return to the earth?"* Too much time has elapsed since the Lord ascended to heaven; Christmas, as the loveliest and most hopeful time of the year, is more likely to be the main item of theological concern during Advent. Are people more apt to listen and respond to sermons on "preparing for Jesus' birth at Christmas" than they are to sermons that declare "prepare for the Day of the Lord?" Yet the Gospels and supporting lessons call for genuine "advent" preaching.

Sermons during Advent should:
1. *Proclaim* the expected return of the Lord some time in the future and *call upon people to take the Gospel seriously and "wake up!";*
2. *Prepare* the way of the Lord by proclaiming the Good News — *He will come again!";*
3. *Present* the claims of Christ — repentance and new life — to his children;
4. *Assure* Christians that they have nothing to fear in the judgment of the Second Coming; they can look forward to Christ's return with confidence and, in the meantime, serve him with joy;
5. *Announce* that the Christ, who was born as a real child at Christmas is actually present as his birth is remembered and celebrated throughout the Christmas season.

Advent "programs" and establishes the preaching agenda for the entire church year when it is properly understood and allowed to influence and determine the theological mind-set of the preacher. Preaching during Advent is a complicated business, at best, but it is of critical importance to the person attempting to "preach through the church year" *to discern the eschatological themes of Advent and to proclaim the fullness of the Gospel* to the faithful people of God.

First Sunday of Advent

Roman Catholic	Isaiah 63:16b-17; 64:1, 3b-8	1 Corinthians 1:3-9	Mark 13:33-37
Episcopal	Isaiah 64:1-9a	1 Corinthians 1:1-9	Mark 13:(24-32) 33-37
Lutheran	Isaiah 63:16b-17, 64:1-8	1 Corinthians 1:3-9	Mark 13:33-37
			or Mark 11:1-10
Common	Isaiah 63:16—64:8	1 Corinthians 1:3-9	Mark 13:32-37

The church year theological clue

Wake up and watch is the biblical/liturgical theme for this First Sunday of Advent. It is a time to think seriously about the promise of the risen Christ to return again to judge, reign, and rule over the earth. There is a "Wake-up!-It's-later-than-you-think!" motif in the biblical fabric of the Advent season, and that note is clearly sounded on this Sunday. Future eschatology is the theological clue supplied by the church year and this First Sunday of Advent.

The Second Coming of Christ is announced in recognition that *he first came as a child,* and that his birth — his *incarnation* — is an accomplished fact. Jesus *was* really born in Bethlehem. No one can deny that. He *arose* from the grave — we believe that — and so the living Lord comes to us constantly through Word and Sacraments, worship and prayer. That Christ has assured us that *he will come again* — we, in our preaching, are to *announce, anticipate, and articulate that glorious return to rule and usher in the fullness of the Kingdom of God.*

The Prayer of the Day

The "stir up" prayer of the classic liturgy for the First Sunday of Advent is appropriate for the readings and worship of the three cycles of the church year. It is a prayer to the living Lord to fulfill the promise made before his ascension — "Stir up your power, O Lord, and come." The prayer is, therefore, a type of Maranatha, the first and *continuing* prayer of the faithful who have taken the Lord at his Word and eagerly anticipate his return to the earth.

The Psalm of the Day

Psalm 80:1ac, 2b, 14-15, 17-18 (R); 80 or 80:1-7 (C, L, E) — This psalm is employed in three different ways by the liturgical churches. The Episcopal Church uses the entire psalm as its first choice; the Roman Catholic Church chops it apart; and the Episcopal (second choice) and the Lutheran Churches cut it in half. In its entirety, it is clearly a psalm of lament, providing a fitting response to the first reading of the day as its refrain-like plea (vv. 3, 7, 18) is raised to God — "Restore us, O God of Hosts [which becomes, "Restore us, O Lord God of Hosts," in v. 18], show the light of your countenance and we shall be saved." The "show the light of your countenance and we shall be saved" thrice-repeated theme also makes an indirect connection with the second reading and the Gospel for the day. Regardless of how the psalm is read — in pieces, in half, or in its entirety — it reflects the situation of the people of God here and now, as well as in the Old Testament times at the beginning of Christianity, when people longed for the salvation of God.

The following verses speak profoundly to the "advent situation" of the people who watched and waited for the appearance of the Lord:

> *Turn now, O God of hosts, look down from heaven; behold and tend this vine; preserve what your right hand has planted. (v. 14)*

> *Let your hand be upon the man of your right hand, the son of man you have made so strong for yourself. And so we will never turn away from you; give us life, that we may call upon your name. (vv. 16, 17)*

The Psalm Prayer (LBW)

> *Lord God, you so tend this vine you planted that now it extends its branches even to the farthest shore. Keep us in your Son as branches on the vine, that, rooted firmly in your love, we may testify before the whole world to your great power working everywhere; through Jesus Christ our Lord.*

(Psalm 80, in conjunction with this prayer would also be appropriate for the Sixth Sunday of Easter in Year A.)

The readings:

Isaiah 63:16b-17; 64:1, 3b-8 (R); 63:16b-17; 64:1-8 (L); 63:16—64:8 (C); 64:1-9a (E)

That the children of Israel have been freed and allowed to return from their exile to their homeland and holy city, Jerusalem, which — with the Temple — lies in ruins, means little to twentieth-century Christians. What really does matter is that they recognized their sinful condition, repented of their sins, and called upon the Lord God to forgive them, to come down from heaven, and to visit them with his mercy and forgiveness restoring them to grace. In their desolation, they realized that they needed more than their holy city and temple; they needed God! Their lament is not ours, however, for most of us "have everything;" — and the emphasis on "things" during Advent and Christmas underlines this truth. In our comfortable and affluent lives, we might admit (in those moments when we are truly honest with ourselves) that we don't really seem to need — or want — God in our world and our lives. The truth of the matter is that we are every bit as spiritually impoverished as the Israelites were. Perhaps we need God even more than they did — and don't know it! Isaiah reminds us of this. He pleads with God to intervene for the Israelites and for us:

> *O that thou wouldst rend the heavens and come down,*
> *That the mountains might quake at thy presence.*

It will probably take divine intervention to save us and our world! We need to have the heavens "rent" by God, not by human beings with their space craft and their missiles, if we are to be saved from sin and ourselves.

1 Corinthians 1:1-9 (E), 1:3-9 (R, L, C)

Paul's greeting to the grace-filled Corinthian congregation, a classic salutation used by many preachers before their sermons — "Grace to you and peace from God our Father and the Lord Jesus Christ" — has a kind of "for all the saints" ring to it. It is followed by his thanksgiving for all the gifts given to them "in Jesus Christ." Despite all that they have been given (teachers and preachers and all kinds of spiritual gifts) they still must wait for the coming and appearance of the Lord, which Paul expected to occur in his lifetime. God will meet all their spiritual needs, sustaining them and keeping them guiltless until that day. Paul believes that God will remain faithful to the community of believers he has created in the name of Jesus Christ. And so, they — and we, too — wait for his promised appearance at the end of time.

Mark 13:(24-32) (E); 13:33-37 (E, R, L); 13:32-37 (C)

Mark is convinced, as was Paul, that the risen Lord will return at a time that even Jesus does not know. There will be an apocalypse — that is certain — and faithful Christians must expect it and be prepared to greet Christ whenever he returns to this world. Mark's parable of the man who left home and left his servants in charge ("each with his work") highlights the fact that the servants must be alert because they don't know exactly when he will return. *But he will return home, and the doorkeeper must be ready to let him in.* But the parable implies that not just the doorkeeper, all of the servants must be ready for their master's return; the tasks that he has given them must be completed by the time he comes home — that is part of their "watching" — and ours, too. The word for the Church of Jesus Christ is "Watch! Expect and be ready for the coming of the Lord!''

A Sermon on the Gospel, Mark 13:(32) 33-37 (R, C) — "It is Always Advent."

1. *An announcement* — Jesus Christ is coming again. Like it or not, he will come and *later rather than sooner — but he will come as he has promised.*

2. *On anticipation* — Contemporary Christians join with all the faithful who have lived out the faith before them in expectation of the return of the Lord. Fear and trembling before the Lord will give way to joy and gladness on that day, for Jesus Christ will claim his own for all eternity.

I often attended a worship service held in a church that has the ancient representation of the risen and reigning Lord in its chancel. Christ, as in the earliest Christian churches, is seated on a throne, surrounded by the angels of heaven. I would like to change that painting — and other classic representations of the Lord reigning in heaven — by changing Christ's position. Instead of having an arm upraised in blessing, I would like to see Jesus' hands placed on the arms of the chair, his body leaning forward a bit as if he were about to rise to his feet, to indicate that the Lord is about to fulfill his promise to his people and come back again. And I wouldn't simply alter this representation for Advent; I would keep the "rising Christ" in front of the faithful all year round to remind them to anticipate the return of the Lord.

3. *On action* — Anticipating the second coming of Jesus Christ demands that the people of God act in the world, doing the work that he has given them to do. The Lord has given us tasks to perform: witnessing where we live and work; doing works of love and mercy in his name; teaching and preaching and baptizing; and, of course, doing the Sunday "work" of "proclaiming his death [in Word and Sacrament] until he comes again."

4. *Our Advent attitude* — Take up the "Advent attitude," the *prayer posture* of the early Christian: "Come, Lord Jesus! Come quickly!" Anticipate Christ's return and engage in those actions that will prepare us for his second coming — as if he were coming, and might come, today!

A Sermon on the First Lesson, Isaiah 63:16b-17; 64:1, 3b-8 (R); 63:16b-17; 64:1-8 (L); 63:16—64:8 (C); 64:1-9a (E) — "Who Needs a Father-God?"

A quarter of a century ago, my wife, daughter, and I were forced to drive out of Berlin, West Germany, through East Germany because the Autobahn that went due west from Berlin had been closed for military maneuvers. We drove to Hamburg, over 100 miles, seemingly under the constant vigilance of East German soldiers. It was a grim ride. The countryside and the towns were stark; we saw few people and fewer farm animals. It appeared almost as though life had come to a stop for these people. One of the most disheartening signs of that time was the number of churches we saw that had not only been closed but had been turned into barns. The last signs of hope in that country seemed to have been obliterated.

A few years ago I had the opportunity to see a major city near where I grew up and where I had even lived for a short time. This was also a disheartening visit, not only because so much of the city had been allowed to run down, but also because so many of the churches had been closed, abandoned, or given over to functions for which they had not been built. Parts of that city seemed like a graveyard to me, and the deserted and dilapidated church buildings were so many gravestones marking the demise of the city and the people who had once lived there. A similar phenomenon is occurring all over our country as people move away, or, worse yet, fall away from their churches.

1. *A secular world* — Any semblance of a holy city in this world is strictly accidental. We have lost the holy city but gained, we think, a secular world, which promises us more than does the City of God.

2. *An unneeded God* — Science and technology, as the tools of a healthy economy and expanding affluence, have almost made God expendable. It is when we really see what we have lost to broken homes, alcohol and drug culture, crime and violence, war and oppression, sickness and death that we begin to understand how much we really do need God.

3. *A repentant prayer* is not the prayer of Isaiah and the children of Israel, who longed for the restoration of things as they were through the forgiveness of their sins, but the genuine prayer of faithful people, who hope for things as they should be.

4. *An authentic plea* — Isaiah offers to put words in our mouths that will guarantee an Advent perspective for our lives and will, at the same time, be pleasing and profitable to God: "Yet, O Lord, thou art our Father; we are the clay, and thou art the potter; we are all the work of thy hand." We dare to add: "Shape us, as you see fit, for your holy purpose in the world." That's the Father-God we really need.

A Sermon on the Second Lesson, 1 Corinthians 1:1-9 (E); 1:3-9 (R, L, C) — "How Long, O Lord?"

A parable of the parousia: A parish pastor, who had devoted his whole life to people and the church, became a seminary professor. One of the young men, whom he had confirmed while he was in parish ministry and whom he had encouraged to prepare for the ministry, went to college, and then entered the seminary where this professor taught. He studied theology for two years, then, to the dismay of his parents as well as this professor, he decided to abandon his theological pursuits. He gave up seminary studies and any intentions he had of becoming a pastor. When his parents discussed the matter with the pastor/professor, he said to them: "I have a feeling that he will return to the seminary and resume his theological education sometime." It took almost twenty years, but that young man did return to the seminary and is about to be graduated and ordained into the ministry of his denomination. The professor, who had discerned the gifts for ministry that the young man had received from God, did not live long enough to see the man resume his seminary career and become a parish pastor; he did not see his prophesy come true.

1. *It was that way with Paul.* He was grateful to God for the Corinthian Christians. He recognized all of the spiritual gifts that God had given them, but he knew that they needed something more — "the revealing of the Lord Jesus," who would sustain them to the end, to the last day.

2. *Paul, like the professor, did not live to see that day* — nor did the members of the Corinthian congregations. We might not live long enough to see Jesus, either — but he will return, as he promised.

3. *The Lord, who has given us gifts for faith and ministry and shaped us into his body the church, will sustain us and keep us faithful to him to the end.* Of that we may be *certain.* We may not be physically alive when he returns, but he will — at the last — return.

Second Sunday of Advent

Roman Catholic	**Isaiah 40:1-5, 9-11**	**2 Peter 3:8-14**	**Mark 1:1-8**
Episcopal	**Isaiah 40:1-11**	**2 Peter 3:8-15a, 18**	**Mark 1:1-8**
Lutheran	**Isaiah 40:1-11**	**2 Peter 3:8-14**	**Mark 1:1-8**
Common	**Isaiah 40:1-11**	**2 Peter 3:8-15a**	**Mark 1:1-8**

The church year theological clue

The Second Sunday of Advent could be called "Preparation Sunday." It points to, first of all, the second coming of Christ, and calls for the spiritual renewal of the faithful. The business of the people who call themselves Christians begins with affirmation of the promised return of the Lord on the last day. It continues, on this Sunday, with our participation in that event — right now — by asking the Lord to make us ready for the coming of the Christ, so that we may further participate in the work of "preparing his way" in the world. That "Christ will come again" was reaffirmed last week (and, if the eucharist is celebrated, will be proclaimed today) but in the prayers, readings, and sermon, the emphasis will be on the preparation of our "hearts" so that we may genuinely celebrate Christ's coming right now. *This is the way — the only way — that will enable us to prepare for the coming of Christ at Christmas.*

The Prayer of the Day

This, the second of the "stir up" prayers, represents a modified reworking of the classic collect for the Second Sunday of Advent. The first of these prayers calls for the Lord to "stir up your power . . . and come," while the second asks the Lord God to "stir up our hearts . . . ." It reads:

> *Stir up our hearts, O Lord, to prepare the way for your only Son. By his coming give strength in our conflicts and shed light in our path through the darkness of this world; through your Son, Jesus Christ our Lord, who lives and reigns with you and the Holy Spirit, one God, now and forever.*

This collect provides specific expression of the theological clue provided by the church year.

The readings:

Isaiah 40:1-5, 9-11 (R); 40:1-11 (E, L, C)

This reading begins with some of the most familiar words in the Old Testament:

> *Comfort, comfort my people, says your God. Speak tenderly to Jerusalem, and cry to her that her warfare is ended, that her iniquity is pardoned, that she has received from the Lord's hand double for all her sins.*

In these few opening verses of Deutero-Isaiah, the prophet, who is speaking to the children of Israel about their restoration after the Babylonian exile (around 538 B.C.) is the bearer of "good tidings," truly a voice "crying out in the wilderness" of their — and our — world. His are the words of hope for a defeated and desolate people, returning to their devastated country. He speaks to this downcast nation, reminding them that they must place their hope in the God of their Fathers, and this indeed, will bring them the comfort they really need — God's' comfort. As a way for God is prepared "in the wilderness," the "glory of the Lord shall be revealed, and all flesh shall see it together, for the mouth of the Lord has spoken." After they have gone through the awful experience of humiliation and suffering in Babylon, the "herald of good tidings" declares to them and "all the cities of Judah," "Behold your God!" God is their comfort and will sustain them in their return and restoration.

There is no indication that Isaiah had in mind Jesus Christ's coming into the world when he wrote these words, but their tone and typology are most appropriate for Advent, in general, and for the Second Sunday of Advent, in particular. It is not surprising that Mark sees John the Baptizer as the "new Isaiah," who is to "prepare the way of the Lord," crying out (as did Isaiah some six-and-a-half centuries before him): "Prepare the way of the Lord, make his paths straight." Just as surely as "Comfort, comfort" heralds the Messiah, so "prepare" suits the role of the Baptizer. John the Baptizer is essentially the "mouthpiece" of God, the "voice" of the one whose mission it is to announce the immanence of the Lord's advent, preaching repentance and baptism for the forgiveness of sins, and thereby preparing the way of the Lord.

2 Peter 3:8-14 (R, L); 3:8-15a (C); 3:8-15a, 18 (E)

Peter, in all likelihood, did not know anything about this letter, nor did he write it; he would have been dead about sixty years when this epistle was prepared. But Peter *might* have said what is in it to counteract the teachings of false prophets and teachers, who apparently were publicly denying the parousia. Almost a century had passed since Jesus' death and resurrection — and he had not returned. Hope of his return was fading; no wonder some people doubted the possibility of his return. So "Peter" corrected such false teachings, reminding the people by quoting a loose translation of part of Psalm 90, "with the Lord one day is as a thousand years, and a thousand years as one day."

The first seven verses of this chapter could be added to the first three verses of today's reading and assigned to the First Sunday of Advent. These ten verses address our situation quite well on the First Sunday of Advent, or any other time for that matter — the second coming of Christ is not a high priority item for contemporary Christians. But the text fits into the theological thrust of this Sunday (beginning with verse 11): the parousia is a present day event in which we participate by repenting of our sins, by seeking to live holy lives, and by living in the hope of "a new heaven and a new earth" brought about by the final intervention of God, rather than wholly by the ingenuity and positive efforts of humankind to improve the quality of life on earth. In other words, this is a matter of living out our baptism in Jesus Christ. This reading complements Isaiah 40 and the Gospel for the Day, Mark 1:1-8.

Mark 1:1-8

Odd, isn't it, that Mark skips all of the details of Jesus' birth and early life and gets right to the point of what he wants to say — that the Promised One has come into the world and is about to be seen and heard? That John the Baptizer was the forerunner of Christ cannot be denied; he spoke like a true biblical prophet, announcing the event that would have ramifications for the world from his time forward. The world would never be the same again, for God, through his intervention and action, had entered the world to change the estate of human affairs forever. This "announcement" was supplemented by John the Baptizer's call for true repentance and baptism for the forgiveness of sins. He did, indeed, prepare the way for the coming of the Lord. He certainly "cried out in the wilderness" of this world, "Prepare the way of the Lord, make his paths straight." He didn't know it when he began to preach, but his ministry would ultimately cost him his head.

John the Baptizer also pointed out that the One who came after him was "mightier" than he, and that there would be a difference in their ministries. He would baptize with water, but the "mightier One" would baptize with the Holy Spirit. John understood — and accepted — his subservient role as a "preparer of the way" for the one "whose sandals," he said, "I am not worthy to stoop down and untie." John's ministry brought a type of judgment to the world, while Jesus offered salvation to all who would believe in him. Perhaps John's different expectations resulted in some believers' disappointment in the mission of Jesus. Fortunately for us, he saw — and participated by baptizing Jesus — the beginning of Jesus' ministry. Unfortunately, he had no way of determining how it would develop. Suffice it to say, he faithfully fulfilled his role in the work of the Lord, and that was sufficient for him then — and for us now.

A Sermon on the Gospel, Mark 1:1-8 — "What's This All About?"

I am certain that if the late Dr. Edmund A. Steimle had been living in John the Baptizer's time and had heard him when he first started preaching, he would have asked one of his favorite questions about biblical stories and events, "What goes on here?" or "What's this all about?" Few people really comprehended what John the Baptizer meant when he declared his mission was to "prepare the way of the Lord" and "make his paths straight." Fewer still, I believe, could even begin to understand him when he said, "After me comes one who is mightier than I, and the thong of whose sandals I am not worthy to untie." Among those who responded to this command, "Repent and be baptized," there might have been complete confusion when he declared, "I have baptized you with water; but he will baptize you with the Holy Spirit." Were their baptisms complete and genuine, or was "John's baptism" merely preliminary to something else? After all, John was a powerful preacher, just as powerful, some believed, as Elijah himself, and when he called on the people to repent and be baptized, they responded. But when he talks about the "mightier One" — and another type of baptism — what goes on here?

1. *John the Baptizer is the very voice of advent — of the coming of the Lord Jesus to the earth to intervene in the relationship between God and human beings.* He spoke the first words of the "Good News," the Gospel of our Lord. What he said was not merely a word about Jesus; it was the Gospel — the beginning of the Good News for the world.

One of the most interesting churches I have ever seen is the Church of the Saints Peter and Paul in Eur, the southern suburb of Rome. It has two large "twin" ambos, or pulpits, one for St. Peter and the other for St. Paul. Peter's ambo has a scene carved on the front of it showing Peter preaching on the day of Pentecost; Paul's shows him preaching in Athens. These scenes reminded me that one thing is missing among many such representations of John the Baptizer in the Church of St. John the Baptist of the Autostrada, just outside of Florence, Italy — a depiction of John the Baptizer on the front of the pulpit with the words, "After me comes one who is mightier than I, whose sandals I am not worthy to untie . . . ." That was his role as a prophet, and he faithfully fulfilled it! For his dedication to his task in the Gospel, we remember him and honor him today. He was, in word and deed, the very forerunner of the Lord.

2. *Jesus' word has reached us, along with John the Baptizer's, and we too, have been baptized with water and the Holy Spirit.* This means that we belong to Jesus Christ, and that we are God's forever. We have not only been "sealed with the Holy Spirit," but we have also been "marked with the cross of Christ forever." Our baptisms *are* valid and complete (although baptism isn't finally completed, according to Martin Luther, until our death); Jesus' baptism was completed on the cross. Salvation is ours — and so is the work of the Kingdom of God. These are two of the reasons that we pray today. "Stir up our hearts, O Lord, to prepare the way for your only Son . . . give us strength . . . and shed light on our path through the darkness of this world" so that we might be faithful to our Lord regardless of what it might cost us (even our heads) in the world.

3. *The business of the baptized is to be faithful to the Lord by participating in the work of the Gospel for which we have been prepared and equipped.* We pray for the Spirit so that we can get on with it — godly living and cross-marked service in the name of our Lord, proclaiming the Advent and presence of the Lord in every way that we can. All who are baptized in the Father, Son, and the Holy Spirit are disciples of the Lord as long as they live.

4. *So what goes on here?* This much we know: with John we are servants of the Gospel and of the Lord. Advent reminds us to get on with the business of being disciples of Christ. He renews us for this — his — purpose.

A Sermon on the First Lesson, Isaiah 40:1-11 (E, L, C); 40:1-5, 9-11 (R) — "The Comfort of God — and 'Couch Potatoes'."

Another memory I have of Edmund Steimle is his induction as Brown Professor of Preaching at Union Theological Seminary in New York City. He spoke about preaching, of course, and the heart of his address was about the biblical content of then-contemporary sermons. Steimle declared that we have been preaching law-gospel sermons long enough, and that it might be timely to put a temporary moratorium upon them. He asserted that people living in the 1960s (he was inducted as chair in 1961) needed to hear a healing and helping Gospel, a Gospel of comfort — "Comfort, comfort my people, says the Lord." His advice to preachers was certainly appropriate for the mid- and late-sixties.

1. *God offers comfort to hurting and suffering people.* He offered it to Israel through his prophet, and he offers the comfort of the suffering Savior to us.

2. *Through Jesus — and his death on the cross — God has pardoned the sins of all people.* Real and lasting reconciliation and restoration to God have been accomplished on the cross of Calvary.

3. *Through Jesus, the Lord God comes with might — and with gentleness and compassion.* For Christ, the Good Shepherd and the living Lord, will feed his own, gather his lambs to himself, and lead his people, like sheep, through life and death itself to eternal life.

A Sermon on the Second Lesson, 2 Peter 3:8-14 (R, L); 3:8-15a (C); and 3:8-15a, 18 (E) — "What Sort of Christians Are We?"

1. Do we really believe that Christ will return, as he said he would? Do we take him at his word, or do we merely dismiss the possibility of the parousia as an improbability, declaring that so much time has elapsed that he will never return to earth?

2. Are we obedient Christians — who really believe him — who seek to live holy and godly lives here on earth, making ourselves pleasing and useful to the Lord while we wait for his second coming? Are we attempting to live out our baptisms in the meantime?

3. Are we informed Christians, who realize that it is necessary to die and to rise — through our baptism — every day of our lives, dying to sin and rising to new life, and so being (as Peter directed his readers) "zealous to be found by him without spot or blemish, and at peace?"

(Note: The problem in developing a sermon from this plan is to avoid preaching a sermon that is law-oriented. Gospel answers to these questions need to be supplied in this type of homily.)

Third Sunday of Advent

Roman Catholic	Isaiah 61:1-2, 10-11	1 Thessalonians 5:16-24	John 1:6-8, 19-28
Episcopal	Isaiah 65:17-25	1 Thessalonians 5:[12-15], 16-28	John 1:6-8
			or John 3:23-30
Lutheran	Isaiah 61:1-3, 10-11	1 Thessalonians 5:16-24	John 1:6-8, 19-28
Common	Isaiah 61:1-4, 8-11	1 Thessalonians 5:16-24	John 1:6-8, 19-28

The church year theological clue

"New Age" Sunday might be one name that could be given to this Third Sunday of Advent. The purpose of this Sunday, which in the older tradition was related to the Fourth Sunday of Lent — "refreshment Sunday," when the spiritual and physical rigors of Lent were relaxed — is that *now* is the time for rejoicing. Christ has come into the world, has inaugurated the Kingdom of God through his death and resurrection. *The New Age has begun,* and therefore, human beings have reason to rejoice.

This Sunday could also be named "Rejoicing Sunday," or as the classic Roman liturgy called it (after the first word of the Psalm) *Gaudete.* (After this tradition, some congregations continue to use a rose-colored candle for this day in their Advent wreaths.) This Sunday, incidentally, has no psalm assigned to it in the Lutheran Book of Worship or the Roman Catholic lectionary. Luke 1:46b-55, *The Magnificat* or "The Song of Mary," replaces the psalm as a responsory to the first reading. (The Episcopal Church also offers the *Magnificat* as an alternate responsory to the Isaiah reading). With Mary, John, and the host of people who believe that Christ *has* come into the world and a New Age, God's Age, has begun, contemporary Christians rejoice and give thanks to God for his wonderful gift in Christ Jesus.

The Prayer of the Day

The *Lutheran Book of Worship* has modernized the language of the traditional collect for the Third Sunday of Advent:

> *Lord, hear our prayers and come to us, bringing light into the darkness of our hearts; for you live and reign with the Father and the Holy Spirit, one God, now and forever.*

It precedes this prayer with a new collect that reflects the John 1 Gospel for the Third Sunday of Advent:

> *Almighty God, you once called John the Baptist to give witness to the coming of your Son and to prepare his way. Grant us, your people, the wisdom to see your purpose today and the openness to hear your will, that we may witness to Christ's coming and so prepare his way; through Jesus Christ our Lord, who lives and reigns with you and the Holy Spirit, one God, now and forever.*

It clearly reflects the intention and themes of the readings for this Sunday.

The Psalm of the Day ("Psalmody")

Psalm 126 (E) — The Episcopal Church has made an appropriate choice when it selected this psalm — a song of rejoicing — as a responsory for the Third Sunday of Advent. It is one of the "Pilgrimage Psalms" sung by the pilgrims as they made their way to Jerusalem and was, no doubt, repeated after they had entered the Holy City and the temple. The people went to Jerusalem because God had restored their nation, so the Psalmist declares: "Then was our mouth filled with laughter, and our tongue with shouts of joy." It has an almost-

Christian eschatological thrust to it from verse 6 onward: "Restore our fortunes, O Lord . . . Those who sowed with tears will reap with songs of joy. Those who go out weeping, carrying the seed, will come again with joy, shouldering their sheaves." The Lord has even greater blessings in store for his people. Christians believe this to be true, so there is real reason for rejoicing.

Luke 1:46-55 (L, E); Canticle 3 or 15 in The Book of Common Prayer; 1:46-50, 53-54 (R)

This glorious song, put in the mouth of Mary by the evangelist, aptly expresses the theme of joy, sung by the church in its liturgy on this Sunday. In an apparent effort to lessen the rather harsh, judgmental themes in verses 51-53, the Roman Catholic Church has skipped over them in this responsory. One could argue that the use of the *Magnificat* on this Sunday gives too much of a Christmas emphasis to the day, and that it throws the sequence of events surrounding the birth of Christ out of order. (Luke 1:26-38, the story of the Annunciation, is the Gospel for the Fourth Sunday of Advent, Series B. The magnificent song that Mary is supposed to have sung on her visit to Elizabeth occurs after the angel visits her and tells her what is going to happen to her.) It is the joyful and thankful spirit of the song that makes it appropriate for this Sunday's worship.

The Psalm Prayer (LBW, Psalm 126)

> *Lord Jesus, our life and our resurrection, the tears you sowed in the sorrow of your Passion brought the earth to flower on Easter morning. Renew the wonders of your power in the Church, so that, after the sorrows of our exile, we may come home to you in gladness and praise you now and forever.*

The readings:

Isaiah 61:1-2, 10-11 (R); 61:1-3, 10-11 (L); 61:1-4, 8-11 (C)

The prophet speaks of the role of the one who is to "prepare the way of the Lord" (the Advent theme in the gospels for these first three Sundays of the season). This person is to proclaim "good tidings" to all of the people, particularly to the poor, the broken-hearted, the captives, and those who mourn, because the One who will come from God will come into the world as a servant. Surely, "Isaiah's" description of the servant's mission fits the life and ministry of Jesus Christ. It is a message of hope for all people, now as well as then.

Verse 10 might have been used by itself as a first reading with its "I exult in Yahweh, my soul rejoices in my God" *(Jerusalem Bible)* to express the liturgical theme for the day's worship. The combination indicates that a new day has dawned, a New Age begun, and God's people — knowing this truth — rejoice and give thanks to the Lord for his love and grace.

Isaiah 65:17-25 (E)

The "New Age" theme, as a reason for rejoicing ("For now I create new heavens and a new earth, and the past will not be remembered, and come no more to men's minds, because I now create Jerusalem 'Joy' and her people 'Gladness'.") comes into prominence in this reading. God has gone into action again, and the Almighty God rejoices over what he has accomplished. There is more than a hint of the Easter joy that brings the incarnation to a culminating look toward the ultimate redeeming activity of God in Jesus Christ — "Behold, I make all things new."

1 Thessalonians 5:16-24 (R, L, C); 5:(12-15) 16-28 (E)

Once more the "rejoice" theme of this Sunday is reiterated in this reading, and this time it is clearly connected to the second coming of Jesus Christ. The thrust of the lesson points to the future when the Lord will return at the end of time. Thus as the various readings suggest, both "advents" of Jesus are amplified on these Sundays of Advent, and faith that the risen Lord will really come again is affirmed as the ultimate reason for rejoicing, praising God for all he has done for his people, and praying the ancient prayer *(Maranatha)* for Christ's immanent return.

John 1:6-8, 19-28

This reading was selected to keep the record right: John the Baptizer was not the Christ — He knew that and simply said so. He was the forerunner of Christ, the herald sent to announce the coming of Jesus into the world. He was not the "light" that would shine in the darkness, merely the one who would testify that a new day was about to dawn with the advent of the Lord. In other words, the Evangelist puts John the Baptizer in his place, in proper perspective: he is not to be recognized as the Coming One. He is merely a "voice" announcing the incredible event that will take place when God enters the world as a human being and takes matters into his own hands. At the conclusion of this reading, John the Baptizer repeats part of last Sunday's Gospel about the presence and the holiness of the Lord — "among you stands one whom you do not know, even he who comes after me, the thong of whose sandal I am not worthy to untie." Thus, the "joy" theme of the Third Sunday of Advent finds expression in the Good News which the Baptizer gives to the world.

A Sermon on the Gospel, John 1:6-8, 19-28 — "Rejoice! There Is Light in this Dark World."

There is a church in Hong Kong called True Light Lutheran Church. I like to think it is a congregation organized on this Third Sunday of Advent — but I'm afraid that was not the way it was. The traditional — and only — Gospel for this Sunday had always been Matthew 11:2-10; John 1 came in with the new lectionary of the Roman Catholic and other churches. Somebody, at least, was intrigued by what John had written in the first chapter of his Gospel about the pre-existent One who came into the world and brought the very light of God to humanity. John the Baptizer clearly stated that he was not that light; he was the one sent by God to prepare the way for the Lord, whose advent was at hand as he spoke. The mission of True Light Lutheran Church — and all other churches and their preachers, for that matter — is to witness to the *True Light, Jesus Christ,* and so proclaim the Good News that the Light will shine in the darkness of this world and give people hope. *Every congregation, into which this Gospel of John is preached, is a "true light" Christian church.*

1. *The man who knew his role in God's world.* John the Baptizer can never be accused of rewriting the script prepared by God for the drama that was to unfold in the life of Jesus Christ. He knew what his task was and he simply accepted the fact that he was a "preparer" and not the Messiah. He didn't take advantage of the response to his preaching — the masses of people, to whom he could have been Elijah or Jeremiah, or even the Messiah himself. *We honor him for his obedience to the will and intention of God.*

2. *We can really rejoice, because we know the true story of Jesus.* John prepared the "way of the Lord" rather than blocked his path or interfered with God's intentions. He was obedient to the will of the Almighty God, and this finally cost him his life. *The light, Jesus Christ, really did come into the world — and so we have abundant life.*

3. *Our joy is enriched by the knowledge we have that nothing could put out that Light. Death could not douse that light, but only dimmed it for awhile.* Jesus, the Light of Life, cannot be extinguished or eliminated from the world by the efforts of evil or indifferent people. The Light is here to stay, and it will shine through the Gospel and the church until the end of this age.

4. *God's Light shines in this dark world and gives us hope and joy!*

A Sermon on the First Lesson, Isaiah 61:1-2, 10-11 (R); 61:1-3, 10-11 (L); 61:1-4, 8-11 (C) — "The Song of a Servant."

1. *The song is composed in "the spirit of the Lord."* It was given to the prophet Isaiah and later to another "singer," John the Baptizer.

2. *The song is sung in loving service of others. The description of Isaiah ("to bring good news to the poor, to bind up hearts that are broken," and so on) is a model for those who would live "in imitation of Christ."*

3. *The song is the song of joyful people.* They know that God is gracious and merciful, and that he has made an everlasting covenant with them in Christ. He has "clothed me in the garments of salvation . . . ."

4. *The song is an expression of faith.* God has promised this — *our deliverance* — and in Jesus Christ he has already made good on his promise.

A Sermon on the First Lesson, Isaiah 65:17-25 (E) — "Never-ending Gladness and Joy."

1. *God is engaged in a new creation in the world.* The prophets understood that God had not given up on his people. Rather than destroying a "sinful world," he set about to recreate it.

2. *This will mean new life for the people of God.* The prophet speaks of "long life" for righteous believers; Christ spoke of "eternal life" for the faithful.

3. *The new creation will bring peace to the earth.* He has promised this with his Word and has accomplished it in the incarnation of Jesus Christ, Isaiah's "prince of peace."

4. *Those who live in this hope will always be glad and rejoice "in the Lord."*

A Sermon on the Second Lesson, 1 Thessalonians 5:16-24 (R, L, C); 5:(12-15), 16-28 (E) — "The Dimensions of Christian Joy."

1. *Fervent worship* — in response to all that God has so graciously done for all people in Jesus Christ.

> *Rejoice, the Lord is King!*
> *Your Lord and King adore;*
> *Give thanks and sing,*
> *And triumph evermore.*

2. *Loving service* — that witnesses to the love of God displayed for the whole world to see on the cross.

> *Jesus, the Saviour, reigns,*
> *The God of truth and love;*
> *When he had purged our stains*
> *He took his seat above.*

3. *Audacious hope* — in the belief that God's will "will be done on earth as it is heaven."

> *His kingdom cannot fail,*
> *He rules o'er earth and heaven,*
> *The keys of death and hell*
> *Are to our Jesus given.*

4. *Eternal expectation* that the Lord will soon return as he promised. Meanwhile,

> *He sits at God's right hand*
> *Till all his foes submit,*
> *And bow to his command,*
> *And fall beneath his feet.*

> *Lift up your heart, lift up your voice;*
> *Rejoice, again I say, rejoice.*
> (Charles Wesley)

Fourth Sunday of Advent

Roman Catholic	2 Samuel 7:1-5, 8-11, 16	Romans 16:25-27	Luke 1:26-38
Episcopal	2 Samuel 7:4, 8-16	Romans 16:25-27	Luke 1:26-38
Lutheran	2 Samuel 7:[1-7], 8-11, 16	Romans 16:25-27	Luke 1:26-38
Common	2 Samuel 7:8-16	Romans 16:25-27	Luke 1:26-38

The church year theological clue

Prior to the revision of the church year and lectionary, the Fourth Sunday of Advent really was "Christmas" Sunday in many Protestant churches. Lections were changed, Christmas hymns and carols were sung, and sermons were oriented toward the celebration of Christmas rather than toward Advent. It was almost as if there were two celebrations of Christmas; people could take their choice of attending one or the other — or both — of the Christmas services. Such practices were a natural outgrowth of interpreting Advent as a time to prepare for "the birth of Christ in our hearts" at Christmas. It smacked of "O Little Town of Bethlehem" theology and had little or nothing to do with the celebration of the presence of the living Lord in the Word and Sacrament at the Christ Mass.

The Fourth Sunday of Advent seems to have perpetuated the liturgical aberrations that often occurred on that Sunday as a kind of "pre-Christmas" celebration. The John 1:19-28 Gospel was assigned to the Third Sunday of Advent, Cycle B, and "Christmas Gospels" were assigned to the three years of the Fourth Sunday of Advent. (They are the stories about Jesus' conception and Mary's pregnancy.) They, with the other propers for the day, turn this into what might be called "Tall Tale Sunday."

The Prayer of the Day

The collect, which is a complete revision of the classic prayer, makes it clear that this Sunday is supposed to be a one-day preparation for celebrating Jesus' birth on Christmas Day. It retains the "stir up" opening — "Stir up your power, O Lord, and come" — but now reads: "Take away the hindrance of our sins and make us ready for the celebration of your birth, that we may receive you in joy and serve you always . . . ." It points the people of God toward the actual Christmas celebration of the church, making it manifestly obvious that the Fourth Sunday of Advent is in no way an early Christmas festival. It reminds us that the only way we can receive Christ at Christmas is through the work of the Holy Spirit in the Word and the Holy Meal, at which the risen and reigning Lord is the Host.

The Psalm of the Day

Psalm 89:1-4, 26, 28 (R); 89:1-4, 14-18 (L); 132, or 132:8-15 (E) — A responsory psalm should perform at least three functions: 1.) It is a vehicle for worship in itself; 2.) It should build a bridge between the first and second lessons; and, 3.) It should highlight and clarify — and sometimes establish — the liturgical theme of the day. Psalm 89 is too long (fifty-two verses) to be used in its entirety for liturgical worship; it has to be cut up and portions have to be excised from the whole to accommodate the liturgical action. It makes a fitting response to the promises that God made to David ("Your house and your kingdom shall be made sure for ever before me; your throne shall be established for ever."). The Psalmist declares:

> *I have made a covenant with my chosen one / I have sworn an oath to my servant David / I will establish your line forever, and preserve your throne for all generations.*

This psalm, as orchestrated by the liturgical committees of Roman Catholic and Lutheran churches may be readily sung or said in worship. It clearly builds a bridge from first reading to those that follow, and it sounds out the theme of the day — "God is about to make good on his promise to David by sending his Son into the world as the Child of a young Hebrew girl named Mary.

The Psalm Prayer (LBW)

Mighty God, in fulfillment of the promise made to David's descendants you established a lasting covenant through your firstborn Son. You anointed your servant Jesus with holy oil and raised him higher than all kings on earth. Remember your covenant, so that we who are signed with the blood of your Son may sing of your mercies forever; through your Son, Jesus Christ our Lord.

Psalm 132 (E) — This psalm, too, functions properly as a responsory, especially when it is trimmed down to verses 8-15 for liturgical worship. It builds a bridge between the readings, picking up where 2 Samuel 7 left off; "The Lord has sworn an oath to David; in truth, he will not break it." Sung by the pilgrims on their journey to Jerusalem for Passover, it anticipates the coming of the Messiah and is particularly appropriate for the conception of Jesus: "A son, the fruit of your body, will I set upon your throne." The "pre-Christmas" theme is definitely delineated in this psalm.

The readings:

2 Samuel 7:1-5, 8-11, 16 (R); 7:(1-7), 8-11, 16 (L); 7:4, 8-16 (E); 7:8-16 (C)

The several lectionaries agree that 2 Samuel 7 is an appropriate reading for this Fourth Sunday of Advent, but they disagree completely on the sections of this chapter which should be assigned to liturgical worship. All four select, as part of their readings, verses 8-11 and verse 16, which highlight Nathan's prophecy to David, received from the Lord the previous night. Nathan makes it clear that David is not to build a house, the Temple, for Yahweh, but that Yahweh will build a "house" for him. The covenant God made with David promises: "Your House and your sovereignty will always stand secure before me and your throne be established forever." In Jesus, the Son of David, that prophecy was fulfilled; his throne shall be from everlasting to everlasting.

Romans 16:25-27

Some scholars think that this doxology is the effort of an editor, rather than the work of Paul himself. At any rate, it was probably selected for this occasion (the Fourth Sunday of Advent) because it complements the theme of preparation for the Christmas festival. God strengthens the faith of his people through the preaching of the Gospel and through Jesus Christ. He has made it manifestly clear that in Jesus the "mystery" that has been kept "secret" about the Messiah, who was to come as David's Son in the name of the Lord, has been clarified forever. He will be made known to all nations, and for all of this God will be glorified. The several lectionaries, incidentally, are unanimous in the selection of this reading for this Sunday.

Luke 1:26-38

Were it not for the existence of various Annunciation stories in the Old Testament, this story would seem to be something out of *Grimm's Fairy Tales*. The story of the angel visiting Mary and informing her that she, a young virgin without a husband, would have a son — would be a bit much for people to believe; it has that "once upon a time" quality to it that signifies, to many people, that "it is only a story." But what a story! It has elements that are occasionally in the Old Testament, such as angels visiting people in their dreams. But the angel not only appears to Mary; he also makes this astounding announcement about Jesus' conception and birth. Luke spins a tall tale, indeed — but for a purpose. Jesus' birth is a genuine incarnation. It is the work of the Lord God, who spoke and formed the world and everything in it, speaking once more and accomplishing through the Holy Spirit a new creation, the Son of God, who is to be given "the throne of his father David . . . . and he will reign over the house of Jacob forever; and of his kingdom there will be no end." God has intervened in human history through the birth of Jesus Christ, and everything is changed forever.

A Sermon on the Gospel, Luke 1:26-38 — "A Likely Story."

Not long ago, my wife and I were traveling on an interstate highway between two major cities. To our dismay, we discovered that it was a truck route and nearly all of the trucks seemed to be traveling seventy- to seventy-five-miles an hour. It was a scary, even hair-raising experience, to have two or three eighteen-wheel monsters (plus some "double-bottom" and "triple-bottom" trucks) thunder past us. At one point, we were literally surrounded by trucks, and one truck came up behind us and almost touched our rear bumper, as if to say, "get out of my way and let me pass." I decided that there was only one thing to do — step on the gas pedal and pull away from them. At the speed I was driving, I suspected that it would only be a matter of time before I was stopped by a police officer, and I knew I had better come up with a good story — soon. So I composed a little speech for any state policeman who might stop us: "Yes, officer, I was speeding; I admit it, and under the circumstances, I would probably do it again. With these trucks practically running over us, *we were really running for our lives,* attempting to protect ourselves from possibly being destroyed by speeding trucks. If you have to give me a ticket for that, I'll be happy to pay it. It's a small price to pay for attempting to save our lives."

Mary, some people might contend, came up with a better story than that when she discovered she was pregnant. She claimed that an angel — she called him Gabriel — told her that God would impregnate her through the Holy Spirit. The angel even supplied her with the name she was to give her child — Jesus — and told her that God would give him the throne of David and that he would reign over an everlasting kingdom. In order to convince her that "with God nothing is impossible," he informed her that her kinswoman, Elizabeth, was also miraculously pregnant in her old age. And Mary finished her story by declaring, "Behold, I am the handmaid of the Lord" — What else could she say to Gabriel?

1. *The Annunciation is a tall tale, but the message of this story is true — God was responsible for Mary's pregnancy!* Could this be one of the reasons that Jesus spoke to God, "Abba, Father?" God didn't simply allow the birth of Jesus to happen in the course of human affairs — *he made it happen!*

2. *Who would believe such a story?* At least, the people who gossiped about Mary's pregnancy — when they got over the shock of hearing that this lovely young girl was going to have a child — must have given her credit for having a lively imagination. At least one person believed her — Joseph. (Matthew tells us that he was visited by an angel in a dream.) Of course, countless people have accepted the story since that time. God wants us to believe that this whole scenario was his idea, his initiative, and, consequently, his incarnate Son, who would be born of Mary.

3. *The living Lord himself visits us to quicken our hearts and to strengthen our faith for the celebration of his birth.* And his story is even more incredible, because he rose from the dead and came out of his grave three days after dying on a cross. That's the tallest tale of all — and the whole Gospel depends upon its truth and validity.

4. *Believe the story and its message.* God has sent his Son into the world, Son of God and Son of David, to save the world. Every bit of it is true!

A Sermon on the First Lesson, 2 Samuel 7:1-5, 8-11, 16 (R); 7:(1-7), 8-11, 16 (L); 7:4, 8-16 (E); 7:8-16 (C) — "David's Dynasty."

King David's dynasty has no resemblance to the popular television soap opera, "Dynasty." It relies on the interest and activity of God Almighty, rather than upon the intrigue and machinations of self-seeking and power-hungry individuals intent upon establishing for themselves and their offspring a power base and some degree of wealth. The word has a totally different meaning in the Bible than it does on the television show.

1. *God revealed his intention to David to bless all people with the inauguration of his kingdom — his dynasty — and to sustain it for posterity.* Such was his covenant, his promise to David and all people.

Almost ten years ago, I heard the story of Eugene Lang, the "venture capitalist" who believed he owed a debt to society, especially to disadvantaged youth, who had no opportunity to go to college. Lang himself had been noticed by a college trustee (Swarthmore), who thought he was too young to be waiting on tables and saw to it that the youthful high school graduate (who couldn't afford a higher education) obtained a full scholarship. Lang succeeded in college and in business. He became wealthy, and gave Swarthmore College $18 mllion. But he still felt that he owed young people more of a debt. He told a class in his first school, PS 121, in New York, that he would send every one of them to college if they studied hard and stayed in school. Later, he realized that he needed to do even more: "A promise can be diluted with time. Even if they stayed in school, the chances are that their education wouldn't be adequate to get them into college. I realized that I would have to provide a program of support to encourage them to stay in school, to help them learn and qualify." He did just that, and the program has become an unqualified success.

2. *In a time, a new king — the Son of David and the Son of God, the Messiah — would appear and assume the throne, the dynasty, of David.*

3. *That Kingdom — that dynasty — will last forever. Nothing on earth can destroy the Kingdom of God, over which Jesus reigns by his death and resurrection.*

4. *Rejoice! The Lord is King. Crown him "Lord of all!"*

A Sermon on the Second Lesson, Romans 16:25-27 — "An Open Secret."

1. *A divine secret was revealed to humanity through the birth of Jesus Christ — God intends to save the world when he really ought to destroy it and start over.*

2. *Through the Gospel of Jesus — and the telling of his story — the plan of God finds expression.* He intends to save the world by sending his Son to die on a cross near a garbage dump.

3. *The same power that raised Jesus from the dead creates faith in human hearts.* The Holy Spirit enables people to believe the unlikely and the impossible, the resurrection of Jesus Christ.

4. *And God strengthens his people, the faithful believers, through this open secret in the Gospel.* Do his work in the world while you await the return of the Lord.

Christmas

Note: A detailed study, with sermon suggestions, is available for the first Christmas service in Cycle A of the *Lectionary Preaching Workbook*. The Roman *Ordo* prescribes three Christmas masses — one at midnight, one at dawn, and one during the day. The Episcopal *Book of Common Prayer* calls its lections Christmas Day I, Christmas Day II, and Christmas Day III. The Lutheran LBW uses the same pattern for Christmas, designating the three sets of readings with Arabic numerals "1," "2," and "3." However, the LBW alters the sequence by placing the readings for the dawn service as number "3." It contains this rubric:

> *Since many congregations have multiple services to celebrate Christmas and since scheduling varies widely, these propers (1, 2, 3) should be employed for the Christmas services (eve and day) as seems appropriate. Traditionally, the first set was associated with the midnight service, the third set with a service at dawn, and the second set with a service later in the morning.*

The readings for the second service (or the Roman Catholic "Mass at Dawn," Christmas Day II [E], A, B, C [LBW] were selected for this study, despite the use of the same Gospel appointed for the first service of Christmas (Luke 1:1-20). Sermon suggestions will be for verses 15-20 of Luke 1.

Roman Catholic	Isaiah 62:11-12	Titus 3:4-7	Luke 2:15-20
Episcopal	Isaiah 62:6-7, 10-12	Titus 3:4-7	Luke 2:(1-14), 15-20
Lutheran	Isaiah 62:10-12	Titus 3:4-7	Luke 2:1-20
Common	Isaiah 62:6-7, 10-12	Titus 3:4-7	Luke 2:8-20

The church year theological clue

Christmas, in the minds of numerous Christians, is the most important festival of the year. That it is the loveliest, no one can deny, but Easter is the pivotal event that the church celebrates in the life of Jesus Christ. Easter and the Great Fifty Days had been observed almost three centuries, before Christmas, one of three biblical and liturgical foci, was separated from Epiphany. Set on December 25, Christmas began a twelve-day celebration signalling the end of Advent, as well as the approach of Epiphany. In time, Christmas became the center of the Advent-Christmas-Epiphany cycle of the church year.

Christmas is a *beginning*, the culmination of God's promise to send a Savior into the world. It is not a baby who comes to believers in the Christmas worship; rather, it is the risen Lord, the Promised One of God, who was born to die — and to rise from the grave on the third day. Recognition of this guarantees that sentimental themes (which often pass for Christmas sermons) will be avoided, and that the pure and true Gospel of the crucified and resurrected Lord will be proclaimed in the context of his second coming, the Parousia. As a climax to Advent, the church may very well pray: "Come, Lord Jesus! Come quickly!"

The Prayer of the Day (LBW)

The classic collect for Christmas Day has been recast in these words:

> *Almighty God, you have made yourself known in your Son, Jesus, redeemer of the world. We pray that his birth as a human child will set us free from the old slavery of our sin; through Jesus Christ our Lord, who lives and reigns with you and the Holy Spirit, one God, now and forever.*

Freedom from sin and its condemnation comes with the cross and resurrection, not with the birth of the Savior. His birth brings the beginning of our salvation, the incarnation of our God as he takes on human flesh in the person of his Son, Jesus Christ.

Psalms 96, 97, and 98 (or parts of these psalms) were selected for Christmas services in Cycles A, B, and C, respectively. Psalm 97 will be considered here; Psalm 96 was treated in the Cycle A Workbook; Psalm 98 will be included in the Cycle C Workbook.

Psalm 97:1, 6, 11-12 (R); 97, or 97:1-4, 11-12 (E); 97 (L) — This psalm is employed for at least two reasons: 1.) It is an ''enthronement'' psalm, which describes what is happening while God reigns in heaven; and 2.) it seems to fit the spirit of the Christmas experience in the birth of Christ — ''Light has sprung up for the righteous, and joyful gladness for those who are true-hearted.'' The concluding verse picks up the refrain of the first verse (''The Lord is king; let the earth rejoice.'') and strikes the same note: ''Rejoice in the Lord, you righteous, and give thanks to his holy name.''

The Psalm Prayer (LBW)

God our King, you clothe the sky with light and the depths of the ocean with darkness. Among the peoples you work wonders, and rain terror upon your enemies. Do not try your servants by fire, but bring us rejoicing to the shelter of your home, where with your Son and the Holy Spirit you live and reign, now and forever.

The readings:

Isaiah 62:10-12 (L); 62:11-12 (R); 62:6-7, 10-12 (E, C)

The liturgical use of this reading takes the celebration of one of the Hebrew festivals and orients it toward the Christmas feast. And, indeed, the heart of the passage fits Christmas very well.

Behold, the Lord has proclaimed to the end of the earth: Say to the daughter of Zion, ''Behold, your salvation comes; behold, his reward is with him, and his recompense before him.''

Titus 3:4-7

This passage highlights the wondrous grace of God in the perspective of the Christmas event. It is all about the goodness and loving-kindness of the God who saved us in Jesus Christ. What we have here is a powerful restatement of the doctrine of justification by God's grace alone, which gets at the very heart of the activity of God to save the world from sin and death. ''The washing of regeneration'' and the renewal in the Holy Spirit bring together the Christmas and the Easter experiences of the church in word, as well as in the Sacrament of the Table.

Luke 2:1-20 (L); 2:(1-14) 15-20 (E); 2:15-20 (R); 2:8-20 (C)

The last section (verses 15-20) of the birth narrative in Luke 2 could have been used as a pilgrimage song for the early Christians who celebrated Christmas in Jerusalem and Bethlehem. Etheria, the Spanish nun who visited Jerusalem late in the fourth century, reported that a three-stage commemoration of Christ's birth occurred in Jerusalem and Bethlehem. The pilgrims walked from Jerusalem to Bethlehem and celebrated the first Christ Mass (around midnight) at the Grotto of the Nativity, the traditional birthplace of Christ. At its conclusion, they returned to Jerusalem and, at the traditional site of the resurrection, participated in the Dawn Mass. Later in the day they gathered once more for the Christmas Day Mass. It would have been appropriate to begin their evening worship with the reading of Luke 2:15-20, or simply verse 15b, ''Let us go over to Bethlehem and see this thing that has happened, which the Lord has made known to us.'' The text also speaks of our own Christmas "pilgrimage" and of our response to this mysterious and miraculous birth. Like the shepherds, we should be "glorifying and praising God for all that they had heard and seen, as it had been told them [and us]." (See also the comments on this passage in the *Lectionary Preaching Workbook, Cycle A*.)

A Sermon on the Gospel, Luke 2:15-20 (R, E) — "Bethlehem by Mercedes Benz."

It struck me as rather paradoxical, when I first visited Jerusalem, that most modern-day pilgrims travelled by tour bus or taxi — Mercedes Benz taxi cabs — from Jerusalem to Bethlehem. True pilgrims should walk that short distance from the city to the small town where Jesus was born, especially at Christmas. But we go to church — by "Mercedes Benz" — to worship the Lord at his birth. We go in automobiles that whisk us in comfort, even luxury, from our homes to our churches. There's an appropriate symbol here (and I recognize that many of us would have to walk all afternoon, or evening, to get to the church by midnight) showing the difference between our situation and that of the shepherds who "went to see this thing that has happened." But there's yet another significant difference: Christmas is "old hat" to us, because we *know* about the birth of Christ. We know who he is, and this ought to inform our worship despite the paradox created at Christmas. *Perhaps we are more like the three Wise Men who went to Bethlehem bearing gifts than like the shepherds. But we can catch the spirit of wonder and joy they all shared. That's reason enough to go to Bethlehem.*

1. *Good news of the birth of the Savior sends us all to Bethlehem to "see this thing that has happened."* God has done something that is spectacular, and our knowing about it is not enough; we must go and "see" for ourselves. (We see with our "ears" and our imaginations as the Word is read and preached and the Christ Mass is celebrated.)
2. *It is not only our mode of transportation that is different; our "Mercedes Benz" mentality may impede and interfere with our worship of the Lord at his birth.* With the Wise Men, we come to Christ bearing gifts for the Christmas offering.
3. *We may not walk to Bethlehem's manger as the shepherds did, but we can give the new-born Savior the best gift we have to offer — ourselves.*
4. *That just might be the gift that pleases Christ the most!*

A Sermon on the First Lesson, Isaiah 62:6, 7, 10-12 (E, C); 62:10-12 (L); 62:11-12 (R) — "An Astounding Announcement."

1. *"Behold, your salvation comes"* — this is God's Christmas proclamation to the world.
2. *Christ, through his loving sacrifice, changes us from sinners into holy people who belong to God — forever.* Christians are the redeemed of the Lord.
3. *Christians always have hope and God will never forsake them.* He is with us in every situation we encounter in life — even death.
4. *Raise the ensign of the Lord — the cross — and put it over the cradle!*

A Sermon on the Second Lesson, Titus 3:4-7 — "Saved by the Grace of God."

Today's newspaper carried the story of the Russian tour ship, the *Maxim Ghorky,* that struck an iceberg between Greenland and Norway. The ship was circling the Singehar Islands at night, while 950 tourists from West Germany were enjoying the festivities, when the crash occurred. Miraculously, as the ship began to sink, there was no panic. The people got into the lifeboats in an orderly manner and they were lowered into the icy sea without incident. A rescue ship arrived inside of three hours and all of the people — every one of them — were saved from a watery grave. Helicopters played an important part in the rescue operation. It was a miracle of grace, because there was nothing — outside of getting into the lifeboats — that these people could do to save themselves. The efforts of others (the crew of the ship and the people who participated in the rescue) actually saved them.

1. *The appearance of the Savior tells the world that God is doing something to save people from sin and death.* The birth of Jesus, his incarnation, was the most radical action that God could have taken.

2. *God did this out of the goodness of his heart — by pure grace — because there was no way that we could save ourselves.* Without the coming of the Christ, we would have been doomed forever, but God sent Jesus to save us.

3. *Therefore, we are heirs of the kingdom that he has brought into the world. Eternal life is ours!*

First Sunday after Christmas

Roman Catholic	Sirach 3:2-6, 12-14	Colossians 3:12-21	Luke 2:22-40
Episcopal	Isaiah 61:10—62:3	Galatians 3:23-25; 4:4-7	John 1:1-18
Lutheran	Isaiah 45:22-25	Colossians 3:12-17	Luke 2:25-40
Common	Isaiah 61:10—62:3	Galatians 4:4-7	Luke 2:22-40

The church year theological clue

The Sundays after Christmas (there may be one or two some years) allow the church time to reflect on "this thing that has come to pass," the birth of Jesus. The few infancy narratives that are recorded in the Gospels put the birth of Christ into kerygmatic perspective. According to Luke, the "Naming" (Circumcision) of Jesus — occurred on the eighth day after Jesus' birth. When this event falls on a Sunday, it is celebrated as a key feast/festival of the church.

In the Roman Catholic *Ordo,* this Sunday is known as "Holy Family Sunday." The Epiphany, concentrating on the Wise Men's visit to Bethlehem to worship the Lord, really brings the Christmas season to its conclusion. However the continuation of that story, which chronicles the Holy Family's flight to and return from Egypt (Matthew 2:13-15, 19-23), is the Roman Catholic Gospel for Holy Family Day (Cycle A). It is also used in the Lutheran and Common lectionaries on the First Sunday after Christmas. *At his birth, Jesus was marked for death; that was the only way his God-given mission could be completed.*

The Prayer of the Day (LBW)

The LBW has a new collect that was composed for use in all three cycles of the church year. It represents a departure from a revision of the traditional collect of the other liturgical churches, speaking of the restoration of "the dignity of human nature," and asking God to "let us share the divine life of Jesus Christ who came to share our humanity, and who now lives and reigns with you and the Holy Spirit, one God, now and forever." It is more appropriate for this Sunday than the traditional Lutheran collect for the First Sunday after Christmas. The collects of other liturgical churches differ considerably in content and theme.

The Psalm of the Day

Psalm 128:1-5 (R) — This psalm, another of the Songs of Ascent connected to the annual Passover pilgrimage, applies the general "family theme" to the Feast of the Holy Family. Those families who "fear the Lord, and who follow in his ways" will, according to the Psalmist, enjoy the blessing of God. At the risk of theological oversimplification, one is tempted to illuminate this theme in the pulpit for the edification of contemporary Christians. The Roman Catholic Church employs it to magnify the Holy Family theme.

Psalm 147 or 147:13-21 (E) — The Psalmist, grateful for all that God has done and is doing in the world, sings this magnificent song of praise to him who is in charge of all things. He praises the God who restored Jerusalem, gathered the exiles, comforted the broken-hearted. This God is "mighty in power" and possesses wisdom that knows no limits. This psalm accommodates the Gospel for the Day, John 1:1-18 *(The Book of Common Prayer)*, calling upon the people celebrating the birth of Christ to worship the God, who through the Word made all things and "became flesh" in Jesus Christ.

Psalm 111 (L) — "You who worship the Lord, obey him and do what he commands in the world" seems to be the theme in this psalm. This could be a carry over from the emphasis made on the First Sunday after Christmas in the traditional collect. That prayer said: "direct our actions according to thy good pleasure, that . . . we may be made to abound in good works." The main reason for using this psalm of praise and thanksgiving surfaces in verse 9: "He sent redemption to his people; he commanded his covenant forever; holy and awesome is his name."

The Psalm Prayer (LBW)

> *Merciful and gentle Lord, the crowning glory of all the saints, give us, your children, the gift of obedience, which is the beginning of wisdom, so that we may be filled with your mercy and that what you command we may do by the might of Jesus Christ our Lord.*

The readings

Sirach 3:2-6, 12-14 (R)

Jesus Ben Sirach would delight at the Feast of the Holy Family; he had his own way of celebrating the family — in piety and obedience. His charge to "children" upholds the Fourth Commandment (or fifth, depending on how one's church counts them) and the place of parents in family life: "Children, listen to me your father, and do what I tell you, and so be safe; for the Lord honors the father in his children, and upholds the rights of a mother over her sons." He does go a bit too far from a New Testament perspective when he declares, "Whoever respects his father is atoning for his sins." However, he is "right on" in saying, "he who honors his mother is like someone amassing a fortune." Since Joseph disappears from the "Jesus Story" before Jesus begins his public ministry, and since Jesus seems to turn his back on his mother at least at one point in his ministry, Jesus Ben Sirach might be put off a bit by the Gospel. But he would certainly applaud what Jesus said (according to John) when he was hanging on the cross: "Woman, behold your son," and to John, "Behold your mother." At the moment of atonement — his baptism — Jesus goes beyond Ben Sirach's instructions and establishes forever a new family, the Family of God that is known as the Church of Jesus Christ.

Isaiah 45:22-25 (L)

This selection from Isaiah emphasizes the First Commandment, "I am the Lord thy God . . . . Thou shalt have no other gods before me," instead of the Fourth/Fifth Commandment. The reading could have begun at verse 21b — "There is no other god besides me, a God of integrity and a savior; there is none apart from me." On this Sunday, which is often in the middle of the Christmas season, the Lord God says, "Turn to me and be saved, all the ends of the earth, for I am God and there is no other." (verse 22) Set in the context of Christmas, and calling for "every knee to bow" and "every tongue . . . swear" (that Jesus Christ is Lord to the glory of God the Father) all people will know that it was God who did this wonderful work through Jesus Christ.

Isaiah 61:10—62:3 (E, C)

This pericope takes up almost where the first reading for the First Sunday of Advent concludes, verse 11. Once more, the Advent/Christmas note of joy is sounded — "I will rejoice greatly in the Lord, my soul shall exult in my God" and "the Lord will cause righteousness and praise to spring forth before all the nations." (verses 10, 11b) It reminds me of TV mini-series which review what happened in the previous episodes before going on with their stories. What follows, particularly in 62:2-3, picks up on the worship theme of Christmas: "The nations will then see your integrity, all the kings your glory, and you will be called by a new name, one which the mouth of Yahweh will confer. You are to be a crown of splendour in the hand of Yahweh, a princely diadem in the hand of your God." *(Jerusalem Bible)* God has indeed done a new thing in Jesus.

(Note: See also the First Sunday after Christmas, Cycle A, for additional comments on this reading.)

Galatians 3:23-25; 4:4-7 (E); 4:4-7 (C)

Comments on these pericopes are to be found in the readings for the First Sunday after Christmas, Cycle A. The Episcopal *Book of Common Prayer* uses the same readings for all three cycles/years of the church year.

Colossians 3:12-17 (L); 3:12-21 (R)

This reading could have been assigned to Epiphany, which was — and is, for some churches — a secondary day for baptisms (if scholars are correct about the "put on," or baptismal, exhortation at the beginning of the pericope). Should this reading have been connected to baptism, it might have referred to the candidates putting on white robes after emerging from the water. However, for most Christians today, it shapes a response to the mystery of Christ's birth — what a Christian should be, as well as what a Christian should do: "and above all these *put on* love, which binds everything together in perfect harmony. And let the peace of Christ rule in your hearts . . . and be thankful. Let the word of Christ dwell in you richly." Christians live in perfect obedience and harmony with the Lord and his Word, because they have "put on Christ" at baptism. Verses 18-21 give specific instructions to members of a family on being a Christian. Although they were in the original version of the LBW lectionary, they have now been eliminated from it.

Luke 2:22-40 (R, C); 2:25-40) (L)

This same Gospel is read on the day dedicated to the Presentation of our Lord. It is ready this Sunday to call attention to the circumcision of the Lord on the eighth day after his birth, and to show that, as a human being, he had to submit to the discipline in the covenant God had made with the Hebrews. He is the Son of God, but he is also a human being and, as a Jew, had to be circumcised. The Holy Family, it should be pointed out, fulfilled its religious obligation to the Lord. But it is the encounter with Simeon and Anna that highlights the reason (beyond the chronological sequence of this episode) for appointing this reading for the Second Sunday after Christmas. Simeon's amazing greeting, known as the *Nunc Dimittis,* and Anna's assertion prophesying Jesus' mission, compel the preacher to tell this part of the story.

John 1:1-18 (E)

See commentary on the First Sunday after Christmas Cycle/Year A.

A Sermon on the Gospel, Luke 2:22-40 (R, C); 22:25-40) (L) — "The Song of a Dying Man."

When an old man committed suicide, his neighbor asked an important question: "Was it an act of cowardice or courage?" Had that man's name been Simeon, one might have been able to give a positive answer to that question. Simeon, once he had seen and recognized the baby Jesus, was ready to die. There's a kind of "Mine eyes have seen the glory of the coming of the Lord" thrust to this old man's song. He was ready to die, but he would never think of killing himself. Were he misguided in any way and eager to enter into eternal life — and had he believed that he had to get to heaven and the throne of God as soon as he could and that this was the way to get there — he surely would have had the courage to do what that other old man did for a totally different reason.

1. *The birth of Jesus opens the way for the destruction of death.* It was the beginning of the process of forgiveness, reconciliation, and the hope of eternal life that God initiated in "the little town of Bethlehem."

2. *The cross of Christ accomplished God's purpose and set people free from the fear of death.* It was for this purpose that he was born. He completed his Father's plan to save all people.

3. *Forgiven and free from the clutches of Satan, sin, and separation from God forever — Christians have genuine hope for the present and the future.* They live in trust and hope by faith.

4. *Completely free, Christians live as the people of God — the redeemed — in this world.*

John 1:1-18 (E)

See the sermon suggestions for the First Sunday after Christmas in Cycle/Year A.

A Sermon on the First Lesson, Sirach 3:2-6, 12-14 (R) — "On Behalf of the Family."

In this age when about half of the marriages that are entered into are dissolved by divorce, when some sociologists are saying that we have seen the end of the family and the home as a place where a family is formed and children are reared with solid values and goals — it seems an empty gesture to devote one Sunday of the year to the remembrance of the Holy Family. Ben Sirach doesn't speak for the Holy Family, but he does have something to say — on this Sunday — to contemporary families.

1. *Sirach was right about family relationships and how they apply to the Holy Family.* ". . . The Lord honours the father in his children." That certainly was the case with the Holy Family; who would ever have heard of Joseph, if Jesus had not been born? And who would ever have seen him as a person of compassion and genuine piety, if he had not listened to and obeyed God? Joseph and Mary, too, found their honor in their Son.

2. *Parents, if they consider themselves to be children of God, have to do their utmost to teach their children the ways of God and rear them in the faith.* According to a pastoral counselor who specializes in family and marriage counseling, the most difficult part of adjusting to a divorce is to help the parents see that each of them has a responsibility in rearing any children caught in this broken home situation.

One of the most tragic situations I have known, found once-loving parents divorced and the husband running off with his ex-wife's best friend. He moved in with "the other woman" — less than two blocks from where his ex-wife lived. His former wife was shattered by the experience, but there was one bright spot in the situation. They both shared responsibility for the rearing of their young son. He lived with his mother one week, and he stayed with his father the next week. He shared both of their lives, and both of them had a constant part in his growth and learning, instead of a few hours on weekends. Despite the break-up of their marriage, their joint parenthood is a model for any home where there are children.

3. *In the home and in the church, children must be taught the true meaning of the Fourth/Fifth Commandment — not only from Ben Sirach's point of view, but also from that of the Gospel.* Jesus honored his heavenly father and could do nothing other than honor his earthly parents. Luke tells us that after Jesus was found in the Temple, he went back home with his parents and "was subject to them." The Gospel teaches us about real love, genuine concern for others, and self-sacrifice. Despite the terrible pain he endured on the cross, he was still concerned with his mother's welfare. That would have made an other man named Jesus — old Ben Sirach — smile.

4. *Jesus respects and honors the institution of marriage, giving his blessing to those families open to his love and gracious instruction.* A Christian home does not save anyone, but it does reflect the fact that its occupants are Children of God, have been "saved" by Jesus, and are attempting to honor their heavenly father by establishing and maintaining a home and family that are pleasing to God. The church furnishes us with a model — and the experience — of what a family, a Holy Family, ought to be.

Isaiah 45:22-25 (L) — "Prelude to the Gospel."

1. *God's call was a prelude to the Gospel* — "Turn to me and be saved, all the ends of the earth."

2. *It finds ultimate expression in the birth — the incarnation — of Jesus Christ.* He came to save people from sin and death.

3. *Paul applied this call to the cross of Christ. (Philippians 2)* He took the words right out of the mouth of Isaiah — "Every knee shall bow, and every tongue confess that Jesus Christ is Lord to the glory of God the Father."

4. *Christmas is the time to hear the call of Christ, to repent and turn to the Lord, and to give him the love, honor, and glory that he deserves in response to the Good News, the Gospel.*

Isaiah 61:10—62:3 (E, C)

See the study and sermon suggestions on this text for the First Sunday after Christmas, Series/Cycle A.

A Sermon on the Second Lesson, Galatians 3:23-25; 4:4-7 (E); 4:4-7 (C)

See the sermon suggestions for these readings in the *Lectionary Preaching Workbook, Cycle A.*

Colossians 3:12-17 (L); 3:12-21 (R) — "A Christmas Response to the Gospel."

1. *Our first contact with Christ came when most of us were infants — at our baptism. At Christmas, we remember the One who came to us as a Savior — at his birth.*

2. *Our baptism is renewed — and the peace of God ours — when we turn to him in true faith with God's Christmas gift list: compassion, kindness, meekness, patience, forgiveness, and above all love.*

3. *A faithful response is possible when we let the Word of God dwell in (us) richly . . . . and whatever we do, in word and deed, (we) do . . . in the name of the Lord Jesus.*

4. *That's a large order for sinful creatures, especially at Christmas, but God will help us become what we should be and do what is pleasing to our Lord.*

The Epiphany of Our Lord

Roman Catholic	**Isaiah 60:1-6**	**Ephesians 3:2-3a, 5-6**	**Matthew 2:1-12**
Episcopal	**Isaiah 60:1-6, 9**	**Ephesians 3:1-12**	**Matthew 2:1-12**
Lutheran	**Isaiah 60:1-6**	**Ephesians 3:2-12**	**Matthew 2:1-12**
Common	**Isaiah 60:1-6**	**Ephesians 3:1-12**	**Matthew 2:1-12**

(Note: The Epiphany of Our Lord seldom occurs on Sunday so that it is not always celebrated as a major festival. It is also one of the festivals which employs the same set of readings for all the cycles/years of the lectionary. The comments that follow are a revised and expanded version of last year's study, including an additional suggestion for an Epiphany sermon.)

The church year theological clue

The liturgical and theological function of the festival of Epiphany is to manifest the full glory of Christ to the world by providing a climax to the Twelve Days of Christmas. When Epiphany moved from the Eastern Church to the Western Church, it became a unitive festival, celebrating Jesus' birth, his baptism, and the first miracle he performed at Cana. Coelius Sedulius' fifth-century hymn, "When Christ's Appearing Was Made Known" (Hymn 85, LBW), illustrates this three-fold nature of the Epiphany. The liturgical revision after Vatican II restored much of the original theological content of Epiphany, concentrating on the birth narrative in St. Matthew all three years. The Wise Men, led by the star, travelled to Jerusalem and Bethlehem to bow before the glory of the Child who was "born King of the Jews." (The same title given him by another Gentile, Pilate, when he turned him over to be crucified).

Liturgical revision has separated the three events — Jesus' birth, his baptism, and his first miracle — and has assigned the baptism and the miracle at Cana to the following Sundays so that on the Epiphany of Our Lord the church may concentrate on the glory of God that is revealed to the world in the birth of Jesus. Subsequently, the First Sunday after the Epiphany commemorates the Baptism of Our Lord. The first miracle at Cana is assigned to the Second Sunday after Epiphany in Cycle/Year C *only*. The problem with this revision is that the *manifestation* — the first and main theological motif of the Epiphany — tends to be lost. The Epiphany festival is not celebrated in most parishes unless it occurs on Sunday. It should be said that the Epiphany theme is picked up in John 1 on the Second Sunday after Epiphany for Cycles/Years A and B. John points to Jesus as "the Lamb of God," while Nathanael says, when he is called, "You are the King of Israel." All of this means that there is an opportunity to *magnify the manifestation of Christ to the world as King of Israel and King of Kings — and to bring the Christmas season to a glorious conclusion.*

The Prayer of the Day

This classic collect has been modernized in language ("nations" instead of "Gentiles," "glory" rather than "beauty," etc.), but retains the basic theme and *evangelical theology* of Epiphany (*"revealed your Son . . . by the leading of a star"*) and its *eschatological thrust* ("to know your presence in our lives" and "brings us at last to the full vision of your glory"). Hence, the collect puts the Nativity and details of the infancy story of Christ into proper perspective by addressing the prayer to the "Lord God."

> *Lord God, on this day you revealed your Son to the nations by the leading of a star. Lead us now by faith to know your presence in our lives, and bring us at last to the full vision of your glory; through your Son, Jesus Christ our Lord, who lives and reigns with you and the Holy Spirit, one God, now and forever.*

The Psalm of the Day

Psalm 72 (L); 72, or 72:1-2, 10-17 (E); 72:1-2, 7-8, 10-13 (R) — This psalm was first used on the Second Sunday of Advent, but for a slightly different purpose. Verse 7 is high-lighted during Advent ("In his time shall the righteous flourish; there shall be an abundance of peace till the moon shall be no more."), but verse 11 is emphasized for the Epiphany ("All kings shall bow down before him, and all the nations do him service."). When these verses are used as antiphons on the Second Sunday of Advent and the Epiphany of Our Lord, respectively, they accent different themes in the psalm by bringing them into sharp relief. The first reveals what the reign of the "king's son" will be like, while the second points out the eschatological scope of his reign. It should also be noted that verses 15-19 are optional in the Advent selection, but the whole psalm is appointed for Epiphany (at least in the Lutheran and Episcopal Chruches).

The Psalm Prayer (LBW)

Almighty God, you gave the kingdom of justice and peace to David and his descendant, our Lord Jesus Christ. Extend this kingdom to every nation, so that through your Son the poor may receive justice, the destitute relief, and the people of the earth peace in the name of him who lives and reigns with you and the Holy Spirit, one God, now and forever.

The readings:

Isaiah 60:1-6

The church has taken this pericope, which originally referred to Isaiah's return from exile in Babylon, and put it into a Christian context. Jesus, to the church, is the "light [that] has come," and in him God's "glory is rising on you [and the whole world]." Christ is the light that shines in the darkness and the One to whom all nations shall come. He has staked his claim in the world; all people and all things are his, *gold and incense* will be brought to him, and the name of God will be praised. After all, it is God who delivered the Israelites from captivity in Babylon, and it is God who sent Jesus into the world to free *all people* from sin and bring to the earth the Kingdom of God. (Note: In the older Roman Catholic missal, as well as some Lutheran lectionaries, this reading was employed as the epistle for the Epiphany. Archbishop Cranmer was probably the first to replace this lesson with a New Testament epistle, Ephesians 3.)

Ephesians 3:1-12

Paul makes the connection clear between Isaiah 60 and the Epiphany. He understands his mission to communicate the Good News of God's revelation and his *Light* in Jesus' advent, and to declare to the "nations" (Gentiles, as well as Jews) that salvation has come through the grace of God in Christ and that it is meant *for all.* Just as John the Baptizer was close to death when he sent his disciples to Jesus asking, "Are you the one who should come, or should we look for someone else?", so Paul was close to death when he sent this letter with one of his disciples to the Church at Ephesus. The difference between them — and both of them died by being beheaded — is that John was (temporarily) uncertain about the identity of Jesus Christ, while Paul was absolutely positive that Jesus was the Christ of God, the long-awaited Messiah. He has not only been party to the establishment of the church, but he has also witnessed the now-elusive unity of the church that brought Jew and Gentile into the Body of Christ.

Matthew 2:1-12

This is the third section of Matthew 2 to be used in the lectionary, but chronologically, it is the very beginning of the Epiphany story. In Cycle/Year A, the second chapter of

St. Matthew (verses 13-18) is read in the worship services with about the same frequency as the pericope for Holy Innocents Day. However, the reading for the First Sunday after Christmas is heard every three years, and is, therefore, treated homiletically more often than the other two parts of this chapter. Matthew incorporates the various signs — the star that led the Magi to Bethlehem, the gifts that they brought and presented to the Child, Herod, — and divine visitations, replete with angels who give warnings and guidance to the Magi and, later, to Joseph. The point of the story is to show how Jesus *is* the Epiphany, God's revelation of himself and his intentions for the entire world.

A Sermon on the Gospel, Matthew 2:1-12 — "The Star that Shines Forever."

Phyllis McGinley, in her *Stones from a Glass House,* published a poem which, despite some biblical inaccuracies, demonstrates that she understands what the Epiphany is all about:

> *In Palestine, in Palestine,*
> *   The flocks unsheltered sleep.*
> *Though night-long still,*
> *On every hill,*
> *   A watch the shepherds keep.*
>
> *And people walk with living fear,*
> *   Lest singing as it fell,*
> *Should shine upon some midnight clear,*
> *   The star that is a shell.*

Hanging on the wall beside my desk is a painting by a former student, Pastor Ron Bock, showing a shepherd on a very dark night with sheep gathered around his feet, his shepherd's crook over his head looking up in wonder at a single bright star in the sky. It is not simply the Star of Christmas, but the Star of Epiphany. Epiphany is real and true — the Star is no "shell" — because God sent Jesus into the world to fulfill his long-standing promise of a Messiah. The same star the shepherds had seen inspired and led the Magi "from the east" to Jerusalem and an audience with King Herod and finally directed them to Bethlehem, where they found the baby Jesus, worshiped him, and gave him gold, frankincense, and myrrh. That it was God's will that they should have a part in this drama receives impetus from God's intervention. By way of a dream, God sent them home by a route that would avoid another meeting with Herod, in order to protect the Christ Child from a jealous, if not mad, despot. Our spiritual stance, for Epiphany and its season, is that of those who *watch, wonder, and worship.*

1. *The Epiphany star is no "shell."* Through it, God beckoned the magi, not merely as *star-watchers who might merely wonder* about it, but also as *travellers* to Jerusalem/Bethlehem to find and worship the child born as "The King of the Jews."

2. *The star continues to shine* — through the Word — in the darkness of the world to light the way out of earth's night into the new day, through Jesus Christ, bringing believers to full communion with God the Father.

> *As a star, God's Holy Word*
> *Leads us to our King and Lord;*
> *Brightly from its sacred pages*
> *Shall this light throughout the ages*
> *Shine upon our path of life.*

(verse 6 of Nikolai Grundtvig's hymn, "Bright and Glorious is the Sky," Hymn 75, LBW)

3. *In the full light of day, the star shines and makes the day brighter* as it reflects the glory of the Lord God in Jesus Christ so that as we worship him, we give him the gift of ourselves.

4. *The church exists as a fellowship of believers who are engaged in a "star trek." They* worship Jesus Christ, their Lord and Savior, but also tell the story of Jesus to others so that the star might shine upon them and light up the darkness of their lives.

(Suggestion: Before doing any work on this sermon, read Arthur Clarke's classic science fiction story, "The Star." In this story, a Jesuit scientist aboard a space ship that has entered a distant galaxy discovers a civilization that has been literally burnt up by its sun. No one had escaped, but artifacts of that beautiful civilization had been stored underground. The scientist stares at a crucifix hanging on the wall and says to God: "There were so many stars you could have used. Why was it necessary to put these people to the fire so that the Star might shine over Bethlehem?" The Jesuit and his companions placed the time of that planet's demise at 4-5 B.C. — they were convinced it was the Star of Bethlehem.)

A Sermon on the First Lesson, Isaiah 60 — "The Son and God's Morning."

1. In Jesus Christ, the light of the Lord has surely come upon the earth; a new day is dawning.

2. Sin has been defeated by Jesus' perfect obedience, but its darkness has yet to be eradicated from the world.

3. As the Good News is told to all people, more and more will turn and "come to Christ," their Lord and God.

4. That great day is coming when everyone who exists will bring gifts to Christ and sing praises to the God who is Creator and Father of all.

(Note: In almost every congregation Holy Communion will be celebrated today. Our "star trek" takes us to the Table of the Risen and Present Lord, where we present our gifts — ourselves — as we worship him.)

A Sermon on the Second Lesson, Ephesians 3:1-12 — "The 'Swan Song' of a Faithful Apostle."

1. The mystery of the Gospel became incarnate in Paul. As a prisoner facing execution in Rome, he sings his "swan song" about the glorious Gospel which has been entrusted to him. He is faithful to Christ, when a word or two of denial could have saved his life.

2. With the revelation of God's mystery in the person of Jesus Christ, the secrets of God's plan of salvation are made known to all who hear the Gospel. Christ came for the sake of the whole wide world — to save all people from sin and death.

3. Through the grace of God, all who believe are made members of the church, the body of Christ. They come to know how great God really is, because they have been marked with his cross and "sealed with the Holy Spirit."

4. Epiphany — the festival of the star and the manifestation of Jesus in the world — teaches us to sing a new song, even a "swan song:"

> *The only Son from heaven;*
> *Foretold by ancient seers,*
> *By God the Father given,*
> *In human form appears.*
> *No sphere his light confining,*
> *No star so brightly shining*
> *As he, our Morning Star.*

The Baptism of Our Lord
First Sunday after the Epiphany
First Sunday in Ordinary Time

Roman Catholic	**Isaiah 42:1-4, 6-7**	**Acts 10:34-38**	**Mark 1:7-11**
Episcopal	**Isaiah 42:1-9**	**Acts 10:34-38**	**Mark 1:7-11**
Lutheran	**Isaiah 42:1-7**	**Acts 10:34-38**	**Mark 1:4-11**
Common	**Genesis 1:1-5**	**Acts 19:1-7**	**Mark 1:4-11**

The church year theological clue

Some times the Baptism of our Lord, or the First Sunday after the Epiphany, functions as the octave of Epiphany. The Epiphany motif is proclaimed once more on this Sunday to make a *theological, rather than an historical, statement.* Jesus is identified by God *as his Son* when he is baptized by John in the Jordan, thereby adding another dimension to the evidence of his identity in the birth narratives of Luke and Matthew. As has been mentioned previously, the festival of the Epiphany had three elements in the Western Church — the birth of Jesus, the baptism of the Lord, and the first miracle he performed at Cana in Galilee. All of the major lectionaries participate in the separation of the latter two biblical themes from Jesus' birth, and all highlight the baptism of Jesus on the Sunday after the Epiphany. The Second Sunday after Epiphany, it will be remembered, finds the miracle at the wedding at Cana assigned to Cycle/Year C only; in the other two years, John's witness to Jesus and the calling of the first disciples at the beginning of Jesus' public ministry are the assigned lections. Portions of chapters 1 and 2 of John (1:29—2:11) are the gospel lections for all three years.

In the baptism of Jesus, there is also an inherent theological statement made about baptism itself. Baptism makes people Children of God — forever. Those who have been baptized in the Name of the Father, and of the Son, and of the Holy Spirit reside in the blessed assurance that they have a heavenly Father, who loves them so much that he sent his Son to save them by dying — *which is the completion of his baptism by John the Baptizer in the Jordan* — on a cross.

The Prayer of the Day

A new collect, or a revision of an older prayer, had to be prepared by several churches for the Baptism of our Lord or First Sunday after Epiphany. They differ very little — but significantly, at times. For example, the Episcopal and Lutheran collects begin almost identically, but the petition differs. The Episcopal prayer reads: "Grant that all who are baptized into his Name may keep the covenant they have made, and boldly confess him as Lord and Savior." The petition in the Lutheran collect prays: "Make all who are baptized into Christ faithful in their calling to be your children and inheritors with him of everlasting life." *The Prayers of the Day are evidence of the "theological fall-out" about baptism. In the Gospel baptism applies to those who have been baptized in the Lord.*

The Psalm for the Day

Psalm 29:1-4, 9b-10 (R) — The Roman Catholic Church assigns this psalm, as it does the readings for the Baptism of our Lord, to all three years of the lectionary. See comments in the *Lectionary Preaching Workbook, Cycle A.*

Psalm 45:7-9 (L) — The LBW lectionary assigns this psalm to the Baptism of Our Lord in all three cycles. Comments on this psalm can be found in the workbook for Cycle/Year A.

Psalm 89:1-29, or 89:20-29 (E) — This psalm is also the responsory for all three years in *The Book of Common Prayer* lectionary; however, it was not included in the workbook for Cycle/Year A. It affirms the covenant that God made with David, "chosen one" of God, to whom he declared, "I will establish your line forever, and preserve your throne for all generations." (verse 3) Verse 20 picks up this theme again, declaring, "I have found David my servant; with my holy oil I have anointed him . . . . My faithfulness and love shall be with him . . . . [and] He will say to me, 'You are my Father, my God, and the rock of my salvation'." (Verses 24 and 26) This exceedingly long psalm (52 verses) finds liturgical utility — and theological "connection" with the readings for this day — in its shorter form. It gets to the heart of the worship for this occasion and eliminates much of the repetition in the complete psalm.

The readings:

Isaiah 42:1-4, 6-7 (R); 42:1-7 (L); 42:1-9 (E)

This reading, also appointed for the Baptism of Our Lord in Cycle/Year A, received consideration in the workbook for that cycle.

Genesis 1:1-5 (C)

The Common lectionary departs from the other lectionaries rather radically in its selection of its first two readings for the Baptism of Our Lord, but employs the same Gospel for the Day, Mark 1:4-11. In the first reading, the first five verses of the creation account are read to emphasize that the God who created all things is doing a "new thing" in the baptism of Jesus, whose life and death will result in a "new creation."

Acts 10:34-38 (R, E, L)

The Roman Catholic, Episcopal, and Lutheran lectionaries assign this reading to The Baptism of Our Lord in all three years/cycles. Commentary can be found in the *Lectionary Preaching Workbook, Cycle/Series A.*

Acts 19:1-7 (C)

As is the custom of the Common lectionary in parts of years A and B, a reading that is not included at all in the other lectionaries has been selected for the Baptism of Our Lord. It differentiates between the baptism of John the Baptizer, with which the disciples that Paul found at Ephesus had been baptized, and that "of Jesus." Paul's explanation of the difference between the two baptisms is that John's was for repentance for the forgiveness of sins. But Paul insisted that people who were baptized should believe in Jesus, for Jesus' baptism bestowed the gift of the Holy Spirit on believers. Subsequently, they were baptized again, received the Holy Spirit, and began to speak in tongues. This reading turns baptism from the person of Christ toward the faithful, assuring the believers that God makes them his children through the same Holy Spirit that came down on Christ at his baptism. It orients the day's preaching toward an interpretation of baptism for contemporary Christians.

Mark 1:4-11 (L, C); 1:7-11 (R, E)

John the Baptizer is portrayed as a prophet/preacher who had a two-part message: 1.) He preached a baptism of repentance for the forgiveness of sins; and 2.) he declared that a "mightier" person than he was coming after him, "whose sandals I am not worthy to stoop down and untie." This One would also baptize — but with the Holy Spirit, not just with water, as did John. His preaching was received with great enthusiasm by the common people and, according to Mark, Jesus himself came to John to be baptized. Nothing is said about whether or not John recognized Jesus as the "mightier One." He simply baptized him. It is unclear whether he saw the dove that descended on Jesus or heard the voice that spoke to him saying, "Thou art my beloved Son; with thee I am well-pleased." Many scholars believe that these were inward experiences of Jesus. This much is evident, however, Mark wanted his readers to comprehend that Jesus, not John the Baptizer, was the Messiah, and that it was in his baptism by the Baptizer that God anointed him with the Holy Spirit and announced — to the world — that Jesus is his beloved Son.

A Sermon on the Gospel, Mark 1:4-11 (L, C); 1:7-11 (R, E) — "The Holy Spirit, Water, and the Word of God."

Local tradition has it that one pastor contacted the parents of newly-born children, inviting them to have their babies baptized in his church by advertising: "Have your baby baptized in this church with water from the Jordan River, where Jesus was baptized by John the Baptizer." Many people responded. He performed thousands of baptisms during his ministry because, for one reason, people believed that the water made the baptisms more authentic than if the children had been baptized with water from an ordinary tap. (I suspect, however, that the unchurched among these mothers and fathers were impressed that this pastor took an interest in them. He called on many of them after they took their babies home from the hospital. More than a few of these people became members of that congregation.) The pastor's theology was, I am certain, better than his "come-on" for baptism. He knew very well that without the Holy Spirit there is no baptism, only water.

1. Jesus was baptized by John with water from the Jordan, but God "anointed" him with the Holy Spirit and the Word. In baptism God always comes to his children in water, word, and the Holy Spirit.

2. This is what makes Christian baptism different from that of John the Baptizer's in the Jordan. God the Father transformed the baptism of John into a Christian sacrament when Jesus was baptized.

3. We, unlike Jesus, the sinless son of God, need to be baptized with the "baptism of repentance for the forgiveness of sins," as well as the assurance that, in our baptism, we have become children of the heavenly Father.

4. Jesus' baptism resulted in his contemplation in the wilderness and his clear call to service and ministry. But his baptism was not completed until he was nailed to the cross and died to save us from our sins. It is that way with us, too, in our baptism.

Luther wrote:

> *Baptism — the dying and drowning of sin — is not fulfilled completely in this life. Indeed this does not happen until man passes through bodily death and completely decays to dust. As we can see, the sacramental action of baptism is over quickly. But the spiritual baptism, the drowning of sin, which it signifies, lasts as long as we live and is completed only in death. Then it is that a person is completely sunk in baptism, and that which baptism signifies comes to pass . . . . Therefore the life of the Christian, from baptism to the grave, is nothing more than the beginning of a blessed death. For at the last day, God will make him altogether new.*

A Sermon on the First Lesson, Genesis 1:1-5 (C) — "Creation — Old and New."

Luther, as the above statement suggests, would be very happy with this choice of reading for the Baptism of Our Lord. Baptism, finally, is the promise of reconciliation with God that will lead to that final day when God will make us new creatures in Jesus. Life, for the Christian, is a succession of deaths and resurrections, which through repentance and faith — and the work of the Word and Holy Spirit — occur every day as long as we live.

1. On the first day of Creation, God created the heavens and the earth and, with darkness and light separated as night and day, set time in motion. Creation is an Epiphany of God.

2. God rewound his time-clock with the birth and baptism of Jesus, because time — through sin and the breaking of the covenant — was running out on the human race. The world needed a new Epiphany.

3. Jesus' baptism — in the Jordan and on the cross — renewed God's covenant with his people, assuring them that they are his and, in light of the resurrection, will be lifted up to new life at the end of time. Baptism is God's new Epiphany.

4. In this life, baptism makes us, as it did Jesus, servants of God and human beings. In loving service we live out our baptisms and engage in God's work of supporting and preserving his creations and his creatures.

Isaiah 42:1-4, 6-7, (R); 42:1-7 (L); 42:1-9 (E)

Homiletical suggestions for preaching from this reading are included in the material for Cycle/Year A of the *Lectionary Preaching Workbook.*

A Sermon on the Second Lesson, Acts 10:34-38 (R, E, L)

See the *Lectionary Preaching Workbook, Cycle/Year A* for sermon suggestions.

Acts 19:1-7 (C) — "A Case for a Second Baptism."

Baptism is a one-time phenomenon. Most denominations agree that a person only has to be baptized once — in the name of the Father, and of the Son, and of the Holy Spirit. Some disputes still exist between those who declare that baptism has to be by immersion if it is to be valid, and those who claim that sprinkling or pouring are equally valid modes of baptism. Some consider baptism an act on the part of human beings wherein they offer and dedicate themselves, or their children, to God. But fewer and fewer churches are demanding that people should be re-baptized when they seek membership in their congregations.

Paul, however, made a case for re-baptizing the disciples he found in Ephesus. They were really disciples of John the Baptizer, rather than of Jesus; they apparently hadn't heeded John's announcement about the "mightier One." Paul straightened them out on that point and proceeded to baptize them with water, Word — and God sent the Holy Spirit to seal them into his Kingdom.

1. Baptism "takes" — and a single, one-time baptism is all that is necessary for forgiveness and deliverance from sin and death — when water, word and Holy Spirit combine in a sacrament of life.

2. Re-baptism is unnecessary, even undesirable. But it is renewed whenever people go to the table of the Lord, hear Jesus' words "This cup is the new covenant in my blood, shed for you and for all people for the forgiveness of sins," and receive his body and blood in repentance and faith.

3. Few of us will speak in tongues, but all of us are given the Holy Spirit — in baptism and its renewal through word, spirit, and sacrament — and called to become witnesses for Jesus Christ in the world, speaking the gospel with enthusiasm and clarity to those who need to hear it.

Second Sunday after the Epiphany
Second Sunday in Ordinary Time

Roman Catholic	1 Samuel 3:3-10, 19	1 Corinthians 6:13-15, 17-20	John 1:35-42
Episcopal	1 Samuel 3:1-10 (11-20)	1 Corinthians 6:11b-20	John 1:43-51
Lutheran	1 Samuel 3:1-10	1 Corinthians 6:12-20	John 1:43-51
Common	1 Samuel 3:1-10 (11-20)	1 Corinthians 6:12-20	John 1:35-42

The church year theological clue

In the "old" lectionary, the Sundays of Epiphany continued the manifestation theme mostly with the miracles of Jesus, beginning of course with the changing of the water into wine at the wedding feast in Cana. This miracle moves to the Second Sunday after the Epiphany, Cycle/Year C, and a new element of manifestation is introduced in Cycle/Year A. Jesus is identified by John the Baptizer, who said, "After me comes a man who ranks before me, for he was before me. I did not know him; for this I came baptizing with water, that he might be revealed to Israel." (Note: The Gospel for the first and second Sundays differs among the various churches. The Roman Catholic Common lectionaries employ verses 29-34 of John 1 for the Second Sunday after the Epiphany, of Year/Cycle A, appointing verses 35-42 for Cycle/Year B. The Episcopal and Lutheran lectionaries have chosen 1:29-41 for A, 1:43-51 for B. Incidentally, the Roman Catholic and Common churches agree on the Gospel selection for this Sunday. The Lutheran and Common lectionaries use the same second reading, and the Episcopal and Common lectionaries agree on the choice of first reading for Cycle/Year B.) Despite these somewhat confusing choices in the readings for this Sunday, in which Jesus is identified (first, by John the Baptizer and then by his first disciples), *the manifestation theme moves into the beginning of Jesus' ministry. His teachings identified him as the Messiah as surely as did his miracles.* Therefore, the Sundays *after* the Epiphany really ought to be called the Sundays *in* Epiphany.

The Prayer of the Day

The contemporary collect that the Episcopal Church has chosen for this Sunday turns the manifestation theme to the people of God as they worship and work in the world:

> *Almighty God, whose Son our Savior Jesus Christ is the light of the world: Grant that your people, illuminated by your Word and Sacraments, may shine with the radiance of Christ's glory, that he may be known, worshiped, and obeyed to the ends of the earth; through Jesus Christ, our Lord, who with you and the Holy Spirit lives and reigns, one God now and forever. Amen*

The task of the faithful is to let the manifestation of the Lord continue in the world through their discipleship. *The Epiphany of our Lord to the world continues today through word and sacrament and the work of the people of God.*

The Psalm for the Day

Psalm 40:1, 3b, 6-9 (R); 63:1-8 (E); 67 (L) — The Roman Catholic Church, along with the Episcopal and Lutheran Churches, employs this psalm for the Second Sunday after the Epiphany, Cycle/Year A (LPW). The comments made therein are pertinent to the readings — and the theme — for this Sunday.

Psalm 63:1-8 (E) — The Lutheran lectionary appoints this psalm for the Twenty-fourth Sunday after Pentecost, Year/Cycle A. Comments on this psalm as a responsory can be found in the *Lectionary Preaching Workbook, Cycle A.*

Psalm 67 (L) — This particular psalm finds multiple usage in the Lutheran lectionary (among others). It functioned as a responsory, for the first time, on the Thirteenth Sunday after the Epiphany, Year/Cycle A. Commentary may be found in the *Lectionary Preaching Workbook, Cycle A*. However, it should be said that the psalm is particularly appropriate to the theme of a continuing manifestation, or epiphany, of Christ in the world through his Word, the Sacraments, and the discipleship of the faithful.

The readings:

1 Samuel 3:1-10 (L); 3:1-10 (11-20) (E, C); 3:3-10, 19 (R)

This pericope tells the familiar story of the calling of Samuel by God. Samuel thought it was Eli who was speaking to him as he slept in the Temple. But each time he was awakened by the voice, Eli told Samuel that it was not he who was calling out to him. But Eli realized after the third "awakening" that it was God speaking to Samuel, and he instructed him to say, "Speak, Lord, for your servant hears you" the next time he heard the voice. That's exactly what Samuel did and said. This story is a type of the calling of Jesus to his mission and ministry in the world in his manifestation, especially when God spoke to him in his baptism. Like Samuel, Jesus responded and began his work of preaching, teaching, and ministering to people in Palestine.

1 Corinthians 6:11b-20 (E); 6:12-20 (L, C); 6:13-15, 17-20 (R)

(Note: The Corinthian correspondence is peculiar to Epiphany. Beginning with this Sunday, it is the second reading for most of the Sundays of Epiphany in all three years/cycles. Most of the readings are from 1 Corinthians; 2 Corinthians is selected for the Seventh and Eighth Sundays after the Epiphany Year/Cycle B [in those few years when there are seven or more Sundays in the Epiphany season]. It is also used in Cycles/Years B and C for the Transfiguration of Our Lord [Lutheran].)

The church at Corinth was infected with the spirit of gnosticism or, at least, with a kind of antinomianism that fostered an "anything goes" — to which the modern adds, "as long as nobody gets hurt" — kind of attitude toward sexual morality. Paul saw this as detrimental to the relationship of the Corinthian Christians to Christ and to each other in the church, pointing out that sexual immorality was, first, a sin against Christ and his church whose "members" we are, and second, that it was a desecration of the body as the "temple of the Holy Spirit." Sexual sin is a rejection of the fact that people are "sealed by the Holy Spirit" in baptism. Sexual sin, then, is a sin against God, who sends the Holy Spirit to us in Word and Sacraments. All of this Paul puts in the context of the cross of Christ: "You are not your own [to do with as you please]; you were bought with a price. So glorify God in your body."

John 1:35-42 (R, C); 1:43-51 (E, L)

The second half of the Gospel for the Second Sunday after the Epiphany (1:29-41), Cycle/Year A in the Episcopal and Lutheran lectionaries, is featured in the Roman Catholic and Common lectionaries today. Comments were made on this entire reading in the *Lectionary Preaching Workbook, Cycle/Year A*. It should also be pointed out that this selection, in the Roman Catholic and Common pericopes, tends to highlight John's identification of Christ before two of his disciples, one of whom was Andrew, the brother of Simon Peter. John declared, "Behold, the Lamb of God!" — and Andrew hurried off to find Simon Peter and said to him, "We have found the Messiah" (which means Christ).

The manifestation/epiphany theme surfaces again in the calling of Philip, to whom Jesus said, "Follow me." He and Nathanael were from Bethsaida, the same town that Andrew and Peter were from. Nathanael had some of the spirit of Thomas in him and had to see Jesus for himself before he would believe what Philip told him, "We have found him of whom Moses in the law and also the prophets wrote, Jesus of Nazareth." Jesus called him "guileless" — and was convinced when Jesus described him and how he saw him under a fig tree. Once more the epiphany/manifestation motif comes out in Nathanael's response: "Rabbi, you are the Son of God! You are the King of Israel." At the end of the encounter, Jesus puts recognition of him as the Messiah in the context of his death on the cross.

A Sermon on the Gospel, John 1:35-42 (R, C) — "Follow-up to a Baptism."

1. The day after Jesus was baptized, according to St. John (who doesn't mention the baptism specifically), *John the Baptizer saw Jesus again and said a strange thing: "Behold, the Lamb of God!"* That was all he said in the presence of two of his disciples. In effect, that's the heart of the announcement in Epiphany: "Behold, the Savior of the world!"

2. *But that was — and is — enough.* They immediately left him and followed Jesus, because they knew now who he really was — and is — the Messiah, the Promised One of God, who is not only to be recognized and revered, but is also to be followed by the faithful wherever he leads. Incredibly, Jesus didn't even ask Andrew and the other disciple of John to follow him; they did it on John's word.

3. Everyone who believes Jesus to be the Lamb of God, who takes away the sin of the world, should follow him without delay. To do less is to reject him.

All baptized Christians are called to "follow" Jesus in whatever way they can. As Paul Tournier says, "We surrender our whole being to the authority of Jesus Christ. This means that we must let God direct us in the use of our body and goods, our work and our money . . . . This means that devotion to Jesus Christ turns over to him not only our inner life but also our social life."

In St. Patrick's Cathedral, Dublin, where he served as dean, a plaque was placed on the wall over his tomb:

Here is laid the Body of
  JONATHAN SWIFT,
    Doctor of Divinity,
Dean of this Cathedral Church,
Where savage indignation
      can no longer
      Rend his heart,
Go traveller, and imitate,
        if you can,
This earnest and dedicated
Champion of liberty.
He died on the 19th day of October,
1745 A.D. aged 78 years.

Swift, I am certain, would tell us to follow and imitate Jesus Christ, as he did.

4. Follow the Lamb, who is our leader — that is always the follow-up to baptism — Jesus' and ours.

John 1:43-51 (E, L) — "Making the most of a Little Evidence."

1. *Most of the disciples remind us of ourselves; Jesus had to call them — directly — and order them to follow him.* That's how it was with Philip, who in turn took Nathanael to Jesus.

2. *Jesus wants disciples, but he particularly desires to have guileless persons, who will be faithful to him and true to their calling, follow him.*

I spent a Sunday afternoon a couple of summers ago in a counseling session with a physician and his wife, who were on the verge of dropping out of the church because their pastor had deceived them — and the rest of the congregation — by becoming involved in an extra-marital affair. He had denied any involvement with this "other woman" in a conversation with the physician, his close friend. Some time later, they joined another parish; a friend of mine was the interim pastor in this parish, but — unbelievably, to me — he became enamored of one of the women in the congregation and literally blew the congregation when people learned about it. Needless to say, that physician and his wife no longer go to, or support, any parish. Perhaps if they encounter a pastor without guile, they will return to the fold once more.

3. *Guileless people mean it when they acknowledge Jesus to be the Son of God, the King of Israel — King of Kings and Lord of Lords. And they will cling to the Lord — with the help of the Holy Spirit — forever.*

A Sermon on the First Lesson, 1 Samuel 3:1-10 (L); 3:1-10 (11-20) (E, C); 3:3-10, 19 (R) — "Listen to the Word of the Lord."

1. *Listen to God when he speaks to you* — Samuel did, John the Baptizer did, Jesus did, and so have the disciples of the Lord for nearly 2,000 years. He *does* speak to you.

2. *Few of us hear voices in the night; few of us hear God speaking directly — in our ears as it were — to us.* There's a contemporary novel about a "hot-shot" college chaplain, who had always done his job efficiently and imaginatively until he suddenly heard God speaking directly to him. The trouble is that, after experiencing this a couple of times, he tells a few people about it. This spread throughout the campus congregation like wildfire. People thought he was a bit strange, perhaps "stressed out." The voices became too much for the people when the pastor, believing that God is speaking to him to work a miracle, tries to restore the sight of a boy who had lost his eyesight in an accident in front of the church. The pastor really has a problem when the miraculous healing doesn't occur and his people hear about it. Sometimes, voices we hear are not necessarily the Voice of God. (Although in Samuel's case — and that of other prophets and saints — the Voice was God's.)

3. *God does speak to us — loudly and clearly — calling us to hear what he has to say and to believe it.* Through his word, he speaks to us. Carrying on a conversation with us in prayer and meditation, he calls us to himself and his work in the world. That's one reason why public and private worship are so important in the life of the Christian.

4. *Listen when he speaks, take in what he has to say in his word, and you will really be confirmed in the faith and in the life and ministry of the Lord.*

By attaching verse 19 to this reading, the Roman Catholic lectionary emphasizes the similarity between Samuel and Jesus as they grew up in the faith. It also underlines the importance of treasuring every word that "comes from the mouth of the Lord." God will accomplish his intentions in what he has said to us through his Word. ("Samuel grew up and Yahweh was with him and let no word of his fall to the ground.")

A Sermon on the Second Lesson, 1 Corinthians 6:11b-20 (E); 6:12-20 (L, C); 6:13-15, 17-20 (R) — "Anything Goes — or Does It?"

1. *Many Christians join non-Christians in the belief that all kinds of sexual activity — marital and extra-marital — are a right to be enjoyed in this enlightened age.* Sex is a matter of "fun and games" — a gift of God to be enjoyed without restriction.

2. *It is amazing that so many people do harm to themselves (with venereal diseases, AIDS, unwanted children, and shattered lives) and to their relationship with Christ.*

A young man said to me recently that he had never seen any reason for getting married. He believed that young people are free to have any and all sorts of sexual activity, including living together without commitment or a marriage covenant. But the time finally came when he realized that he ought to marry the girl he was living with. His conscience seemed to get the better of him, and he thought that he and his fiancee should be married in a garden. He said to his disappointed mother and father, who wanted them to be married in a church, "I don't want a church wedding, because I don't deserve to be married in a church." As has happened with so many others in similar circumstances, he had drifted away from the church. His religion with Jesus Christ had been ruptured by his sin, and he thought it to be virtually unforgiveable.

3. *Quite often, the whole church is affected, even hurt, by the moral failures of people — particularly the leaders, ordained or lay, of congregations.* When those who are supposed to set an example of obedience in living the new life in Christ for others, flaunt the teachings of the Word and live as they please, the results are predictable and *terrible.*

4. *All of us are expected to glorify the Lord — in our bodies — by what we are and what we do. This eliminates entirely the "enjoy yourself/anything goes" mentality of those who call themselves children of God.*

Third Sunday after the Epiphany
Third Sunday in Ordinary Time

Roman Catholic	Jonah 3:1-5, 10	1 Corinthians 7:29-31	Mark 1:14-20
Episcopal	Jeremiah 3:21—4:2	1 Corinthians 7:17-23	Mark 1:14-20
Lutheran	Jonah 3:1-5, 10	1 Corinthians 7:29-31	Mark 1:14-20
Common	Jonah 3:1-5, 10	1 Corinthians 7:29-31 (32-35)	Mark 1:14-20

The church year theological clue

Those who look at the lectionaries for the remainder of Epiphany will notice that the semi-continuous reading of the Gospel of St. Mark begins on this Sunday, skips over Lent and Easter, and resumes on the Second Sunday after Pentecost. The rhythm of these readings is interrupted for five Sundays in the middle of Pentecost (the tenth through the fourteenth Sundays), when John 6 is appointed as the Gospel for the Day. *This, incidentally, is the only time that the Gospel of St. John is read in consecutive, or semi-consecutive, order — and this despite the fact that John is the appointed Gospel almost as often as Mark during Year/Cycle B.*

The significance of this is that on this Sunday the theological clue begins to shift from the church year to the Gospel for the Day (and the other readings). But during Epiphany the influence and theological impact of the church year is really stronger than it is in Pentecost, throwing its frame around these lections from Mark and continuing to proclaim the manifestation theme in the beginning of the ministry of Jesus. The theological clue for this Third Sunday after the Epiphany is simply that *when Jesus called the first disciples, they followed him without question, recognizing his uniqueness and divine origin.* He was someone special to them (although it would take considerable time before they fully knew his identity and understood his mission).

The Prayer of the Day

The collects for this Sunday vary from church to church, but they tend to reflect the Gospel and to apply it to the situation of the churches today, asking God to empower his people by the Holy Spirit to proclaim the Good News faithfully and effectively in the world. *The Book of Common Prayer* puts the beginning of Jesus' ministry and the calling of the disciples — and us — in the "manifestation perspective:"

> *Give us grace, O Lord, to answer readily the call of our Savior Jesus Christ and proclaim to all people the Good News of his salvation, that we and the whole world may perceive the glory of his marvelous works; who lives and reigns with you and the Holy Spirit, one God, for ever and ever. Amen*

The Psalm of the Day

Psalm 25:4-9 (R) — This is the prayer of a person who has repented of his/her sins, has turned to God for mercy, and has asked God to enable him/her to be obedient to the will of God. Verses 8 and 9, which make an appropriate response to the first reading, are the key verses in this responsory: "He guides the humble in doing right and teaches his way to the lowly. All the paths of the Lord are love and faithfulness to those who keep his covenant and his testimonies."

Psalm 130 (E) — *De Profundis* is assigned to this Sunday partly because it reflects the situation of Jonah that is suggested in the first reading, but also because it magnifies the mercy and love of a God who is willing and ready to forgive the transgressions of his people when they turn to him and repent of their sins. It is not simply a Song of Ascent sung by the pilgrims on their journey to Jerusalem, but it is a psalm that speaks hopefully in the very face of sin and death. It could have come out of the mouth of Jonah after he had been thrown into the sea (later in the story). He had no hope without divine intervention and deliverance — nor does any other person.

Psalm 62:6-13 (L) — This psalm, in its entirety, functions as a responsory for the Eighth Sunday after the Epiphany in the Lutheran lectionary in those rare years when there would be nine Sundays after the Epiphany. By beginning at the sixth verse of this psalm, Jonah's situation after answering God's call and heading for Nineveh is portrayed graphically and beautifully: "For God alone my soul in silence waits: truly, my hope is in him." God is not only the hope of the Psalmist and Jonah, but of all people, even today.

The Psalm Prayer (LBW)

Lord God, in a constantly changing world we look to you as our rock of hope. Hear us as we pour out our hearts to you, and give us grace and secure protection; through your Son, Jesus Christ our Lord.

The readings:

Jonah 3:1-5, 10 (R, L, C)

Jonah had a mission — that's what the story is all about, despite the fact that the "great fish story" comes to mind when Jonah's name is mentioned. God called him to go to Nineveh and preach to the people to repent of their sins and turn to Yahweh, who is Lord and God of all. God wanted to turn the prophet into a missionary, which did not go down very well with Jonah. He didn't want to go to Nineveh and preach to the Ninevites; he wondered why God would want to save those Gentiles. As a result, when he put out to sea he wound up in the belly of the "whale" and spent there three days and nights — seen by Matthew and others as a representation of Jesus' death and resurrection. His preaching, when he finally reached the city, was effective. The people "proclaimed a fast, and put on sackcloth, from the greatest of them to the least of them." And God forgave them their sin and evil and did not punish them as he said he would.

Jeremiah 3:21—4:2 (E)

It is readily apparent, when one reads this book, why Jeremiah was a very unpopular prophet; his prophesies, in reality, almost cost him his life. He spoke out boldly against the sins of Israel, calling for repentance and renewal, at a time when the Kingdom of Judah was coming to its end. He also told the people that they would be rejecting the will of Yahweh if they resisted the might of the army that was about to invade their land and the Holy City. He speaks for Yahweh: "Come back, disloyal sons, I want to heal your disloyalty." Hence, there is a call to repentance in this reading which parallels that of Jonah's powerful call in the first reading of the other churches. There is also the promise from God himself that he will receive them and bless them — and make them a blessing to others — when they do return to him.

1 Corinthians 7:17-23 (E)

On the first reading of this pericope, it sounds as though Paul was simply answering questions about marriage and sexual relations that the Corinthian congregation had asked him. Perhaps he was attempting to prevent some type of revolt or insurrection against their rulers and (slave) owners. But what he is really getting at in this section of the chapter is that God has given all people gifts for service and ministry, and he wants them to know that God has also *called* them to ministry. He urges them — and us, too — to answer that call. They were not to worry about unimportant details that might or might not be related to the faith. Instead they should be concerned about doing the will of God in their world.

1 Corinthians 7:29-31 (R, L); 7:29-31 (32-35) (C)

In this reading, Paul reveals why he has advised the Corinthians to acknowledge the commands of God and to answer the call of their God to obedience and service. Paul believes that the end of the world — with the return of the risen Lord — is at hand. The parousia is to take precedence over everything else in their lives; they are to concentrate their thoughts and efforts upon preparing for the coming of the Christ. Jesus' second coming should be their "number one priority" as they await the return of Christ. Thus, this reading builds a bridge between the first reading and the Gospel for the Day. (It would also be very appropriate for the First Sunday of Advent.) A new and better world will come into being when Jesus comes again. The Christians already live in the "beginning of the Kingdom" — now they are to await its fulfillment in the parousia of the Lord.

Mark 1:14-20

Mark understands Jesus' preaching, at the beginning of his ministry, from the perspective, that "God is doing a great thing" in Jesus; the Messiah, along with the kingdom promised in the Old Testament, has come into the world and God has inaugurated a new age. Jesus' preaching took up where John the Baptizer left off. He declared: "The time is fulfilled, and the kingdom of God is at hand; repent, and believe in the Gospel." Although the content of Jesus' message contains this note of repentance, he was really calling upon the people to believe in him as the Promised One of God. This is a far cry from the Baptizer who said, "I am not the Christ . . . . I am the voice of one calling in the wilderness, 'Prepare the way of the Lord, make his paths straight' . . . . One comes after me whose sandals I am not worthy to stoop down and untie." Jesus believed that he was that one — and that was the Good News he proclaimed to his hearers. *Jesus' preaching was a manifestation — an epiphany — of our Lord.*

Mark also tells his version of the calling of the disciples by Jesus in the second part of this text. He saw Peter and Andrew as they were fishing and called them to follow him and to become "fishers of men." They, along with James and John, dropped everything, abandoned their vocations, and immediately went with him. *Christ's epiphany was real to them. It was God's manifestation of himself in the Christ and to the world.*

A Sermon on the Gospel, Mark 1:14-20 — "A Tale of Two Families."

(Note: This might be one of those Sundays on which I would preach one of those *occasional* types of sermons, which could be entirely in the form of a story or parable. People have heard before how they, too, are called to discipleship, but they need to hear it again, especially if the preacher has been doing anything to interpret the meaning of their baptism in their lives. *Baptism means that we are all called to follow Christ and become ministers of the Good News in the world.*

1. Two families that I have known for thirty years have had the same Gospel preached to them by the same pastors. They have the same number of children (five), have attended church regularly, sung the same liturgy and hymns, said the same prayers, and even stood side-by-side at the communion table, but they live worlds apart from each other, although they have similar incomes and on the surface, at least, somewhat comparable life-styles.

2. One family, however, seems to be disintegrating — emotionally and spiritually. It has experienced alcoholism, drug use, unemployment among the children, divorce, and currently one member of the family is in jail for aggravated assault. In a recent letter, that young man — after a visit from a pastor of his denomination — said, "I've made an awful mess of my life; I've just about lost everything — and now I've lost my freedom. I guess I just didn't listen, especially in church. I hope it's not too late to turn things around." Two of the other young men in that family are not much better off. In a way, *the call of the world was louder and clearer to this family than the call of the Lord.*

3. The other family is utterly amazing; parents and children are contributing members of society, engaged in one way or another with the business of living out and spreading the Good News. Their Christmas letter is one I look forward to with anticipation. (They have recently moved away.) One son has given up his surgical practice to become a medical missionary. Another son has become a teacher on the mission field. Two of the daughters are nurses, one in Africa, the other in Southeast Asia. The youngest girl is finishing school and plans to become a social worker. It is very obvious that the members of this family, have not only heard and answered the Gospel, but have also responded to their parents' lead. (He is a physician and she is a nurse who spend time every year engaging in medical missionary work in various parts of the world.) *To them, the call of Christ is louder than the call of the world!*

4. *Christ continues to call all of us today through the Gospel and in our baptism.* He gives all of us sufficient grace to answer that call in faith and obedience. He says to everyone, "Follow me!" That's really Good News, isn't it?

A Sermon on the First Lesson, Jonah 3:1-5, 10 (R, L, C) — "A Powerful Preacher"

1. At the mention of Jonah, people immediately remember his brief sojourn in the belly of a whale; he ought to be remembered, primarily, as an obedient prophet and preacher of the Lord.

2. His preaching brought an entire city to its knees; he knew how to preach the law — and repentance. The power of his preaching was in God's word.

3. The people responded as all people should when they hear the word of God; they responded with true faith and they turned from their evil ways to God's way of righteousness.

4. God did what he always does when people hear and heed his word; he blessed them, as he has blessed us.

Jeremiah 3:21—4:2 (C) — "God's Call — People's Answer."

1. *God called long ago — and God is calling now.* He calls us, much as he called the children of Israel: "Come back, disloyal men, I want to heal your disloyalty." He calls us to the cross of Christ for our healing.

2. *They answered — as we should:* "We are here, we are coming to you, for you are Yahweh our God." Jesus really is important in our lives, for he is the Son of the Almighty God — and our Savior.

3. *God directs:* "Do away with your abominations and you will have no need to avoid me." He welcomes us into the Kingdom of his Son, where he will abide forever.

4. *He makes us a blessing to all people — in our Lord, Jesus Christ.*

A Sermon on the Second Lesson, 1 Corinthians 7:29-31 (R, L); 7:29-31 (32-35) (C) — "The Sky is Falling."

1. *That's how it appeared to Paul;* the sky was about to fall and Jesus Christ was about to return to bring in the fullness of the Kingdom.

2. *Christ's return may or may not be imminent, but we live in a rapidly changing world.* God seems so far away and so unnecessary, at times — so desperately needed at other times. Isn't this an age that drops its "Come, Lord Jesus! Come quickly!" in favor of "Lord, have mercy upon us"?

3. *As faithful Christians, our business is to respond to his word in hope and obedience.* In the belief that he is always with us and will see us through all things to the blessed victory he has won for us.

1 Corinthians 7:17-23 (E) — "Paul on Christian Living."

1. *Christians are different.* God expects his people to live differently from those who do not acknowledge him as Lord and God.

2. *Christians are to follow the lead of the Lord* — and to reject pride and greed, which make them dissatisfied with their lot in life.

3. *Christians live gratefully* — for they know that "they have been bought and paid for" by Christ at the Tree. They give God thanks in every way they are able.

4. *Christians live expectantly* for they have been freed from sin and death, and are slaves to no one. They glorify their father by living in faith, hope, and love.

Fourth Sunday after the Epiphany
Fourth Sunday in Ordinary Time

Roman Catholic	**Deuteronomy 18:15-20**	**1 Corinthians 7:32-35**	**Mark 1:21-28**
Episcopal	**Deuteronomy 18:15-20**	**1 Corinthians 8:1b-13**	**Mark 1:21-28**
Lutheran	**Deuteronomy 18:15-20**	**1 Corinthians 8:1-13**	**Mark 1:21-28**
Common	**Deuteronomy 18:15-20**	**1 Corinthians 8:1-13**	**Mark 1:21-28**

The church year theological clue

The Epiphany — the manifestation of the person of Jesus as the One promised by God — continues on this Sunday and determines the choice of readings, including the Gospel for the Day. Despite the fact that the *lectio continua* (or semi-continuous) reading of the Gospel has taken over, the Epiphany theme still determines which specific selections will be read (and, generally, preached upon). As he did in the miracle at the wedding feast in Cana, Jesus continues to identify himself and manifest his uniqueness in his ministry by his teaching and his miracles. The Gospel for the Day bears this out, because the people in the synagogue at Capernaum that day were amazed at his authoritative teaching and his ability to heal a madman with a word. The end of that pericope remarks, ''And at once his fame spread everywhere throughout all the surrounding region of Galilee.''

The Prayer of the Day

The LBW prayer is basically a reworking of the classic collect for the Fourth Sunday after the Epiphany. (See, for example, the *Service Book and Hymnal* or the *Common Service Book.)* Its wording suggests that the language of the older collect has simply been modernized and brought up to date, instead of being informed by the Church year/season theme or the Gospel for the Day. Once more, the Lutheran propers reveal that a different collect is needed for almost every Sunday of the three-year lectionary, if there is to be thematic agreement between the several parts of the propers. And while some of the newer, or reconstructed, collects may fit the texts better than others — such as the prayer in the *Book of Common Prayer* for this Sunday (''Almighty God, you govern all things both in heaven and on earth: Mercifully hear the supplications of your people, and in our time grant us your peace . . . .'') — many, if not most of them, have little or no bearing on the content of the readings.

The Psalm of the Day

Psalm 1 (L) — This psalm is also appointed for the Fourth Sunday after the Epiphany, Cycle/Series A. Commentary on it is located in the *Lectionary Preaching Workbook, Cycle A*.

Psalm 95:1-2, 6-9 (R) — The Roman Catholic lectionary selects this psalm for two other liturgical occasions, the Third Sunday in Lent, Year A and the Twenty-third Sunday in Ordinary Time (plus two Sundays in Year C). The *Venite* is taken from this psalm, although some key verses (3-5) are passed over in this selection. In this liturgical setting, it responds to the first reading in the invitation to Israel (and to people today) to: ''Come, let us bow down and bend the knee, and kneel before the Lord our maker. For he is our God, and we are the people of his pasture and the sheep of his hand.'' Verse 7b is very timely in this age (''Oh, that you would hearken to his voice'') because it focuses on the problem that preachers have whenever they mount the pulpit — how to get people to listen to and to heed the Word of the Lord God. ''Harden not your hearts,'' declares the Psalmist, ''as your forebears did in the wilderness . . . .''

> *Almighty God, neither let us go astray as did those who murmured in the desert,*
> *nor let us be torn apart by discord. With Jesus as our shepherd, bring us to enjoy*
> *the unity for which he prays; and to you be the glory and the praise now and forever.*

Psalm 111 (E) — This psalm of thanksgiving, which contains a recitation of the faithfulness of God to his covenant with Israel and spells out "the deeds of the Lord," is one of many psalms that might have been appointed as a responsory to the Deuteronomy 18 reading. It is quite appropriate for use with this set of lections.

The readings:

Deuteronomy 18:15-20

A cursory reading of this text reveals why it was chosen as the First Reading for this Sunday. It speaks to Jesus' authoritative teaching in the synagogue at Capernaum, as though to indicate that Jesus is the prophet — the "ultimate" prophet — promised by God in Deuteronomy 18. The prophesy of John the Baptizer is interpreted in the scripture as penultimate, which he himself recognizes in saying that One will come after him and is now at hand, whose sandals he is not "worthy to stoop down and untie." Of course, Jesus not only spoke like that "promised prophet," as he vividly described the Kingdom of God whose fullness was yet to be seen, but he revealed himself to be the One by whom it was being initiated in his life, his teachings and ministry, and in his death and resurrection. This is a splendid selection to complement and point to the Gospel for the Day.

1 Corinthians 7:32-35 (R)

Here is one of the most suitable passages in the New Testament for developing an argument for a celibate clergy, both male and female (or as in the Roman Catholic Church, priests, lay brothers, and nuns). Unmarried clergy *can* put all their time and energy into their clerical vocation when they have no family ties or complications. They *can* invest themselves totally in the work of the pastoral office. Such wisdom can hardly be challenged from one point of view but there are numerous arguments, which need not be listed here, for a married clergy. Paul's opinion in this matter doesn't carry much weight with people today (and I suspect that few preachers would prepare and preach a sermon from this perspective on this text). But Paul's point is that celibacy is a gift of God given to a few, who then are able to give up the good estate of marriage to engage in the even "greater work" of God in the world.

1 Corinthians 8:1-13 (L, C); 8:1b-13 (E)

In this age of Weight Watchers, Nutri Systems, and Ultra Slim Fast diet programs, Paul's discussion of eating the food offered to idols, and thereby causing another person "to fall" (from the faith), falls on deaf ears. The idolatry of which he speaks now takes the shape of overeating and downright gluttony — or it may just be, in the United States, part and parcel of an affluent society. Most people are not able to eat well at home, but they are able to dine at restaurants — or the fast food outlets — one or more times a week. Self-satisfaction is the idol that many persons worship and seek to satisfy; good food and fine wines are becoming idols in themselves. Eating and drinking become idolatry when they are engaged in — at any cost — without any thought of, or concern for, the underprivileged people of the world who are hungry all of the time. Our business may not be so much to prevent other persons from falling, but to feed the hungry and starving people on this planet.

Mark 1:21-28

On his first visit to Capernaum, Jesus went into the synagogue where he had worshiped many times before and really began his public ministry there. Two things happened: First, the people were *astonished* at his teaching, because he taught them with *authority*; and, secondly, they were *amazed* at the power he had and the *authority* in his speech that enabled him to perform an exorcism on the man who had been "possessed by a demon." Jesus needed only to say that authoritative word to exorcise the demon and restore the man to normality. This combination — of teaching and miracles — made his ministry an immediate success. "His fame spread everywhere throughout all the surrounding region of Galilee." In Jesus, God broke into time and this world, as he said he would, in the teacher who came to save all of the children of God.

A Sermon on the Gospel, Mark 1:21-28 — "Beating Satan at His Own Game."

In June of 1989, the newspapers carried a story about a person, Simone Sotteau, who had been writing "poison pen" letters to the people of her town (Villereu, France) for almost a decade. It took most of that time to discover her identity, confront her, and, upon her confession, charge her with several crimes. Her vitriolic letters, which were sent to neighbors, friends, public officials, and anyone else who offended her in any way, were, in the words of her priest and confessor, "The work of the Devil." She seemed to be "possessed," and had a dual, Dr. Jekyll/Mr. Hyde, personality. In public, she was an agreeable, pleasant, and caring person, who contributed to the good of the town. But in private, she turned into a demon and wrote her awful letters to the townspeople, even to her husband. She signed her letters with an open threat: "Someone who will get you one of these days."

She was caught through the efforts of a young detective, Daniel Mihls, who had been appointed to the case in 1988. In about one year, by following various leads which led him to Simone, he was convinced that she was the "poison pen writer," so he set a trap and caught her. He had discovered that the letter writer misspelled certain words, one of which was F-L-I-C, a slang word for police in French. He gathered a group of people, including Simone, and asked them to write sentences in which the word appeared. She was the only one who misspelled the word. Police raided her home, arrested her. Under pressure, she admitted to having written one letter, finally breaking down and confessing to all of them. Her "premeditated violence," as her crimes were called, carried penalties of fines up to $3,000 and a maximum penalty of two years in prison. Some people thought she was innocent, others thought she worked with another person, and some were convinced that she was guilty. One townsperson commented, "One thing is sure. We've not heard the last of *Le Corbeau,*" as Simone was called. Perhaps if the priest had been correct and she had been demon-possessed, an exorcism of some sort or other would have been necessary.

1. *As astonishing as Jesus' teaching was, his exorcism of the demon-possessed man was absolutely amazing.* He demonstrated that the authority event in his teaching was also resident in his person. He had the power — the authority — to cast out demons from people.

2. *Jesus revealed, therein, that he was not only the final prophet, of whom the writer of Deuteronomy spoke, but that he had come to set things right for God in the world.* By driving out the devil in the man in the synagogue, he revealed that God had declared war on Satan, and that God would ultimately defeat Satan through Jesus.

3. *Jesus' exorcism in the synagogue at Capernaum provides a preview of the defeat the Devil would experience in the death and resurrection of the Lord.* As he had done on numerous occasions in his life, Jesus turned back Satan when he was crucified. His "obedience unto death" was the final defeat, an exorcism that would eliminate the Devil as a force against God in the world.

4. *Jesus has beaten Satan at his own game.* That means that Jesus, the risen Lord, will return as he has promised, in God's time to accomplish that last victory and bring in the fullness of the kingdom, which he claimed for God when he died at Calvary.

Deuteronomy 18:15-20 — "The Ultimate Prophet."

1. Early in the history of Israel, the need for the final prophet who will speak to the world all that God commands him to say is evident.

2. His word will carry the very authority of God Almighty. God himself will be speaking to the people through this prophet.

3. God will condemn those who take lightly, or reject, the word he speaks through this prophet. God will eliminate any false prophets.

4. That promised prophet has entered the world in the person of Jesus Christ. Listen to him, heed his word, and live.

A Sermon on the First Lesson, 1 Corinthians 8:1-13 (L, C); 8:1b-13 (E) — "Salvation by Consumption."

Visit a Shinto temple in any Oriental city after a funeral has taken place and you may actually see what it was that concerned Paul when he wrote this part of his first letter to the Corinthian congregation. The family and other mourners bring gifts of food for the deceased and leave them before the idols of their faith. People could quite easily, in some temples, steal the food and eat it — perhaps in the mistaken belief that such "consecrated" food would insure the blessing of long life, even eternal life. Is that so different from the medieval practice of not consuming the consecrated Bread at the communion, but taking it home, revering it by placing it under one's pillow or some other place where it could bring the ultimate blessing to the faithful?

1. *Superstition saves no one.* Nobody can be saved "by bread alone, nor is there — or will there ever be — water that comes from a "fountain of youth" that will guarantee a kind of eternal youth, everlasting life.

2. *Salvation comes through the word of God* — that is the food and drink people need to gain eternal life. We are fed "by every word that proceeds out of the mouth of God" and are satisfied by his Word.

3. *Savor the sacrament, the meal Jesus established to remember him, and celebrate the victory he achieved on our behalf.* We can't eat our way into heaven, but his meal — body and blood, bread and wine — sustains us as we go.

1 Corinthians 7:32-35 (R) — "Balancing Act."

Some years ago, a group of Roman Catholic seminarians and one of their professors, had dinner with my wife and me in our home. At the time, the celibate/married clergy question was in the minds of many people, and the discussion about this issue prompted one seminarian to remark: "It doesn't really matter to me whether or not priests are allowed to marry; I have chosen to follow the celibate way of life; because it is the way that I believe I can best serve Jesus Christ." He believed that his vow of chastity and celibacy would solve the problem of balancing one's obligations to God in a clerical vocation against one's responsibilities to family and friends in this life. If Andrew Greeley's fiction *(The Cardinal Sins)* is true to the lives of many Roman Catholic clergy, the "balancing act" is not easy to accomplish. (Note: The married diaconate of the Roman Catholic Church speaks to the problem, but may complicate the "balancing act" for some clergy.)

1. *There is tension between living in the world and living in the Kingdom of God for all of us.* We attempt to do a "balancing act" between our obligations to family, job, community and our responsibilities as citizens of the Kingdom of God.

2. *Put priorities in proper order.* "Seek first the Kingdom of God and his righteousness," Jesus said, "and all will be added to you." Our problem is that we tend to "seek the other things" first — and only *then* do we seek the Kingdom of God. The "balancing act" has to go in God's favor, or else it results in disaster.

3. *When God comes first in our lives, the "balancing act" is rejected and discarded.* Life is seen and lived in proper perspective — that of the cross of Christ.

Fifth Sunday after Epiphany
Fifth Sunday in Ordinary Time

Roman Catholic	**Job 7:1-4, 6-7**	**1 Corinthians 9:15-19, 22-23**	**Mark 1:29-39**
Episcopal	**2 Kings 4:(8-17) 18-21 (22-31) 32-37**	**1 Corinthians 9:16-23**	**Mark 1:29-39**
Lutheran	**Job 7:1-7**	**1 Corinthians 9:16-23**	**Mark 1:29-39**
Common	**Job 7:1-7**	**1 Corinthians 9:16-23**	**Mark 1:29-39**

The church year theological clue

The Epiphany/Manifestation theme — "this is the Promised One, the very Son of God" — continues to be announced at the beginning of Jesus' ministry, not by direct identification by God, nor by the disciples or other people; the works that Jesus does, and what he teaches, show the world that this One is different from other people. Jesus' ministry and preaching, as the reading of the story in the Gospel for the Day suggests, gives evidence to the world that he is the Messiah, whom God promised to save his people. By this time in the Epiphany season, the church year depends on the readings, especially the Gospel for the Day, to sustain and amplify the manifestation of Epiphany that shows plainly to the world that Jesus is the Son of God.

The Prayer of the Day

The contemporary collect in the LBW is a fitting prayer for this Sunday and its Gospel for the Day, which tells a "tall tale" — to many persons — about the things Jesus did and was able to do at the very beginning of his ministry. He not only entered the world, but he came with the power of God at his disposal; he used that power for the good of human beings, healing all sorts of diseases and illnesses and, especially, "driving out demons." The prayer reads:

> *Almighty God, you sent your Son as the Word of Life for our eyes to see and our ears to hear. Help us to believe with joy what the Scriptures proclaim, through Jesus Christ our Lord.*

The Psalm of the Day

Psalm 142 (E) — This could have been Job speaking in his misery and desolation. The psalmist, too, went through an experience of extreme anguish and pain, much like Job's, and cried out his complaints — and his pleas — to God. He says to God, "You are my refuge, my portion in the land of the living." He is isolated from all other people, can count on no one but God to give him help and deliver him from his "prison" of suffering and pain, so he calls upon God — his only hope — to remove his pain and anguish and set him free again.

Psalm 147:1-6 (R); 147:1-13 (L) — In this post-Exilic psalm, which was probably composed after the walls of Jerusalem had been rebuilt (verse 2), the psalmist offers praise and thanksgiving to God for all that he has done. He recites a list of things that God has done for the people of Israel, which reminds us of the ways that he has blessed us, too. His God is maker and ruler of heaven and earth, a creator who cares for his creation and his creatures. The Roman Catholic reading concludes with a positive statement about God's redeeming activity on earth: "The Lord lifts up the lowly, but casts the wicked to the ground." The longer reading of the Lutheran Church ends on a note of praise: "Worship the Lord, O Jerusalem; praise your God, O Zion." This psalm was, no doubt, selected for this Sunday's responsory to engender the spirit of thanksgiving and praise time the people of God for all that he has done for them. It would be appropriate on any Sunday.

The Psalm Prayer (LBW)

God our Father, great builder of the heavenly Jerusalem, you know the number of the stars and call each of them by name. Heal hearts that are broken, gather those who have been scattered, and enrich us all from the plenitude of your eternal wisdom, Jesus Christ our Lord.''

The readings:

Job 7:1-4, 6-7 (R); 7:1-7 (L, C)

''Nobody knows the trouble I've got'' could well have been the song of Job, had he been able to sing; he couldn't, because he was in too much anguish and pain. He lost virtually everything he had, his ''flesh was covered with worms; (his) skin hardens, then breaks out afresh . . . . My days . . . come to their end without hope . . . . my eye will never see good again.'' Job, like most of us, thought he deserved better treatment at the hand of God; his righteousness did not get him the blessings he thought he deserved from the Lord, but in the end he learned his lesson about the grace and goodness of God. Apparently, this pericope was selected because it pictures the miserable estate of people when Jesus began to preach and heal, pointing to the fact that Christ came to preach and teach — and die, too — and his healing ministry was an act of pure grace, mercy, and compassion. The reading does provide something of a background for the setting of the Gospel for the Day.

2 Kings 4:(8-17) 18-21 (22-31) (32-37) (E)

A portion of this pericope was assigned to the Sixth Sunday after Pentecost (the Fifteenth Sunday of the Year) in the Roman lectionary; comments upon it may be read in the *Lectionary Preaching Workbook, Cycle A.* The short form of this text (vs. 18-21) tells the story of the Shunamite woman who, with her husband extended their hospitality to Elisha, whom she called ''a holy man of God,'' by building him his own room on the roof of their home. Elisha rewarded her friendship and graciousness by telling her that she, who had no children, would bear a son in her old age; she did. Now the infant has grown into childhood, gets a severe headache out in the field with his father, is taken to his mother and dies. She places him on Elisha's bed, and leaves the room. The longer version continues to relate the story of how she tells her husband to get a ''servant and one of the asses, that I may go quickly to the man of God, and come back again.'' She says to him, ''It will be well.'' And of course, it was. After an extended discussion with Elisha, he sends his servant to lay his crook upon the body of the boy; he does, but the child does not awaken. Elisha himself visits the home and miraculously resuscitates the dead child and gives him back to his mother. She, like some of the people who were healed by Jesus, fell to the ground and worshiped him.

1 Corinthians 9:16-23 (E, L, C); 9:15-19, 22-23 (R)

This text makes one realize that the recent expose of the financial machinations of some of the TV evangelists is not new at all. Paul, so that he may be all things to all people, will accept no money for his ministry among the people of the Corinthian congregation; he does not want to be accused of preaching the gospel simply for the sake of the money, or of desecrating his ministry by using it for personal gain. He knows that he has been called by the Lord to preach the Gospel of the crucified and risen Savior of the world, not the story of a magician or a man who came to work miracles and, thereby, attain a comfortable way of life, even affluence, by being a ''false prophet.'' He was convinced that God had called him to preach, and he knew the content of the message he was expected to deliver in the name of the Lord Jesus Christ.

The beginning of Jesus' ministry was marked by teaching and healing. The content of his teaching in the synagogue at Capernaum was not reported, possibly because the miracle he performed there — driving out the demon from the man who was "possessed" — seemed to overshadow, rather than confirm, his authority and power. At any rate, that miracle and the healing of Simon Peter's mother-in-law, coupled with the healing of people with all sorts of diseases and the casting out of demons, makes the Christ primarily seem to be a miracle worker at the start of his public ministry. But Jesus will not allow his mission to be viewed from that perspective and, after he was almost "mobbed" by people seeking cures and miracles, told the disciples, "Let us go on to the next towns, that I may preach there also; for that is why I came out." Mark reports, "And he went throughout all Galilee, preaching in their synagogues and casting out demons."

A Sermon on the Gospel, Mark 1:29-39 — "Jesus — Magician or Messiah?"

In his interesting book, *Jesus the Magician,* Morton Smith writes:

> *"Jesus the magician" was the figure seen by most ancient opponents of Jesus; "Jesus the Son of God" was the figure seen by that party of his followers which eventually triumphed; the real Jesus was the man whose words and actions gave rise to these contradictory interpretations.*

Smith asks, "What then were the marks of a magician?" First of all, he had to do miracles. He was primarily a miracle worker. In the synoptic gospels, it is Jesus' exorcisms that lead scribes to say, "He has/is Beelzebul," and "He casts out demons by the ruler of the demons." Morton Smith also mentions that opponents — such as Celsus — in their explanation of Jesus' career, claimed that Christ went to Egypt as a hired laborer, acquired "experience of some (magical) powers," returned, "proclaiming himself a god on account of these powers." " 'Powers' in Greek," he writes, "means both the powers and the miracles done by them." The beginning of Jesus' ministry demonstrates that he had power — and that he performed miracles.

1. *Was Jesus merely a magician or was he really the Messiah?* That people were attracted to him because he could work miracles — had the power to heal — is undeniable. Healing services today will attract great crowds of the curious, as well as those seeking miraculous cures. For people — then and now — he is a miracle worker, a magician, if you will.

2. *Magician or Messiah?* Jesus knew who he was and why he had come into the world. He also knew he had the power to heal; he used that power to cure illnesses, correct infirmities, and to drive out demons, but he was aware of the danger he faced when his ministry featured magic and miracles. He did not want to be known as a magician, because he knew himself to be the Messiah. The Heavenly Father had revealed his identity to him: "You are my beloved Son, in whom I am well pleased."

3. *Messiah, not magician* — that knowledge initiated his preaching/teaching ministry in Palestine. He employed his "power" — his authority — in his preaching and teaching — and people continued to be amazed at his teaching. He did not simply preach the Word; it became evident that he was the Word "became flesh and dwelling among us."

4. *Messiah* — that's how he comes to the world and to us. He does release his power into our lives, supporting us in all situations in life, but he uses his power, primarily, if not exclusively, to save people — even us.

A Sermon on the First Lesson, Job 7:1-7 (L, C), "Job — The Patient Man."

1. Job — the model for every person who has experienced undeserved suffering. Few people believe they deserve the pain and anguish they receive in life. Long ago, I stood by the bed of a man who had been operated upon for cancer; the surgeon, who performed the surgery, was there, too, and said to the man, "It was a malignant tumor, but I believe that we got all of it." The cancer patient, who had wasted his life in many ways and had hurt people in the process, replied, "I deserved it." Most people are more like Job and can't understand what is going on when tragedy comes into their lives and ask, "Why is this happening to me?"

2. Job suffered — not in silence, but in faith. He spoke out and described his situation in which time had reversed itself. Night was interminably long; daylight was all too short. Surely he described his situation — ours, too — but he suffered in faith, never giving up on God.

3. Job's patience and endurance did not win him deliverance from his suffering; that came as a gift from a loving and gracious God. In time, the God who came to the earth in Jesus Christ will rescue all of the people from pain and death. With Job, we can count on that!

2 Kings 4:(8-17) 18-21 (22-31) 32-37 (E)

The "sermon suggestion" that appears in the study for the Sixth Sunday after Pentecost, *Lectionary Preaching Workbook, Cycle A*, deals with the first portion of this story, and leaves the second part of the table for this Sunday. The story highlights the "manifestation" in this story; Elisha, indeed, is "a holy man."

1. A man of God — in word and deed. Elisha came with the same kind of power and authority that Jesus had, but he was not the Messiah, and, like John the Baptizer centuries later, he knew it.

2. A gracious guest — he responded immediately to the Shunamite woman's need, sent his servant, and — finally — went himself to raise up her dead son (At this point, the story connects with Jesus' delay in going to Bethany in the death and raising of Lazarus.)

3. The powerful presence — Elisha, alone in the room with the dead child, raised and restored him to life by the power of God. God's powerful presence was in that room — and that presence is available to all who need it and call upon Christ for it. He will raise up all believers at the last day.

4. God's powerful presence comes to us — not through Elisha, but through Jesus Christ.

A Sermon on the Second Lesson, 1 Corinthians 9:16-23 (E, L, C) — "Paul's Imperative — Preaching."

1. Called and committed to the preaching of the word — Paul was convinced that the Gospel had to be proclaimed, and that he was called to do just that. Preaching the Good News was an imperative for him.

2. He became a *Servant of the Word* (Farmer's title for a book on preaching). Paul did what every faithful preacher of the Word must do; he made himself subservient to the Lord and his gospel. He did what he had to, and became what ever sort of person was necessary, in order to preach the Word with power.

3. He preached the Word freely — literally — rejecting any financial support from the Corinthian congregation so that they would comprehend that Christ and the Gospel took precedence in his life. His preaching was authentic (See Arndt Halvorson's book, *Authentic Preaching*) — because he was authentic (and would have been even if he had been paid for preaching). It takes authentic preachers and authentic people to proclaim and witness to the Gospel of the Lord Jesus Christ.

4. God makes us authentic people — as he did Paul — through the gift of his Word and faith and lays on us the imperative of witnessing to his Word today.

Sixth Sunday after Epiphany
Sixth Sunday in Ordinary Time

Roman Catholic	Leviticus 13:1-2, 44-46	1 Corinthians 10:31—11:1	Mark 1:40-45
Episcopal	2 Kings 5:1-15	1 Corinthians 9:24-27	Mark 1:40-45
Lutheran	2 Kings 5:1-14	1 Corinthians 9:24-27	Mark 1:40-45
Common	2 Kings 5:1-14	1 Corinthians 9:24-27	Mark 1:40-45

The church year theological clue

In the pre-1970 church year, this would probably have been one of the *gesima* Sundays, partly because there could only be six Sundays after the Epiphany, and this only when Easter came late in April. The orientation of this Sunday would be more toward Lent than Epiphany. But in some of the churches, the Sixth Sunday after Epiphany would have a Transfiguration orientation, which provided a fitting climax to Epiphany with its "This is my beloved Son" identification of Jesus by God the Father. That event on the mountain also builds a bridge from the Epiphany season into Lent.

There is virtually no echo of the Voice that announced in Jesus' baptism on the First Sunday after Epiphany, "You are my beloved Son; with you I am well pleased," evident in this seldomly observed section of Epiphany; it is necessary to turn to the Gospel for the Day to discover the Epiphany emphasis upon the manifestation of Jesus Christ as the Promised One of God. Once more, it is an infirm person who begs Jesus for relief from, in this case leprosy, who becomes the occasion for the revelation that Jesus has the power of God to heal and the mind of God to have mercy upon a sick and miserable outcast from society. The works that Jesus was able to perform, in response to the needs of people, manifested his divine nature to those who were healed and all who witnessed those deeds. *Jesus let his gracious actions toward people identify himself in a profound manner as the Son of God.*

The Prayer of the Day

New collects for this and the remaining Sundays in the Epiphany season had to be prepared by some of the liturgical churches, because the collects for this Sunday are related to the Transfiguration of the Lord. The new collects are oriented toward knowing the will of God and responding to God's will in obedient action. For example, the collect of the *Book of Common Prayer*, which is a reworking of a classic collect, reads:

> *O God, the strength of all who put their trust in you: Mercifully accept our prayers; and because in our weakness we can do nothing good without you, give us the help of your grace, that in keeping your commandments we may please you both in will and deed; through Jesus Christ, our Lord . . . .*

Once more, it becomes obvious that if there are to be three sets of lessons, and if the Prayers for the Day are to be in harmony with them, three sets of prayers will need to be composed. Rather obliquely, in the confession "in our weakness we can do no good without you," the prayer expresses a positive response to the Gospel for the Day. Specifically, those who have experienced the grace of God as the leper did (Mark 1:40-45), should become evangelists for the Lord who manifests his nature in his healing ministry.

The Psalm of the Day

Psalm 32 (L, R) — Two portions of this psalm speak to the manifestation theme — Jesus' cleansing of the leper — in the Gospel for the Day. One declares (vs. 7, 8): "Therefore all the faithful will make their prayers to you in time of trouble . . . . You are my hiding-place; you preserve me from trouble; you surround me with shouts of deliverance." Later in verse 11, the psalmist says "Great are the tribulations of the wicked; but mercy embraces those who trust in the Lord." The leper had begged Jesus on his knees, "Lord, if you will, you can make me clean." Jesus did.

Psalm 42 (E) — This very familiar psalm speaks to the condition of the leper in today's Gospel: "Why are you so full of heaviness, O my soul? And why are you so disquieted within me?" The leper had good reason for having a "heavy soul," but he reacted to his malady — and his opportunity in the presence of Jesus — to the psalmist's advice: "Put your trust in God." He did — through his plea to Jesus — and, accordingly, was restored to full health. This psalm, which has baptismal overtones, does complement the Gospel for the Day quite well.

The Psalm Prayer (LBW — Psalm 42)

Lord God, never-failing fountain of life, through the saving waters of baptism you called us from the depth of sin to the depths of mercy. Do not forget the trials of our exile, but from the wellspring of the Word satisfy our thirst for you, so that we may come rejoicing to your holy mountain, where you live now and forever.

The readings:

2 Kings 5:1-4 (L, C); 5:1-15 (E)

This is the familiar story of the Syrian military man, Naaman, who had leprosy and, had he been a Jew, would have been banished from society and sentenced to shouting, "Unclean! Unclean!" as long as he lived. But he was informed, by the Hebrew slave girl to his wife, that he should seek out the prophet Elisha, who had the power to heal him. A letter from the King of Israel provided him with entre to Elisha, who invites him to his home, but doesn't see him when he gets there. A servant of the prophet tells him to go to the Jordan and wash; furious over Elisha's failure to see him and the cure that is proposed; Naaman flies off in a huff. Lucky for him, his advisers convince him to obey the word of the prophet; he goes to the Jordan, washes himself seven times, and he is healed. He was *clean* once more, as clean as the leper Jesus healed in today's Gospel.

Leviticus 13:1-2, 44-46 (R)

This chapter of Leviticus spells out all the gory details of the fate of any person who contracted any sort of a skin disease, especially leprosy. These excerpts from the chapter reveal that such people had to go to the priests for diagnosis and, if they were diagnosed as lepers, pronounced unclean. Their fate was exile from society and the worship of the temple, allowing their hair to grow long and hang down, wearing torn clothing, and going around shouting, "Unclean!"

The combination of these two readings helps to comprehend the situation of the leper who begged Jesus for healing, as well as Jesus' response of not only healing the man but sending him back to the priests who had condemned him in the first place. Both might find a place in a sermon on the Gospels for the Day.

1 Corinthians 9:24-27 (E, L, C)

Paul's familiar image of the Christian life, as the running of a race in which only one person may win, is meant to assure believers that faithful Christians will be "winners" in the Kingdom of God; they will receive an "imperishable crown" when this life — the race — is finished. Thus, what he says, particularly about the discipline involved in the running of this race, suggests that the Christian might realize the proximity of Lent and get ready to "get in shape" — that is, to engage in the rigorous and penitential spiritual exercises of Lent — and be strengthened to keep the faith all of his/her life. The reading has little or nothing to do with the other lessons.

For some reason or other, the Lutheran commission which originally adopted this passage from the Roman Catholic *Ordo* for the Sixth Sunday in Epiphany dropped it in favor of the above reading, but the Roman lectionary retains it. Two portions of one verse — "do all to the glory of God" and "that of many, they may be saved" — give it some homiletical utility in conjunction with the Gospel for the Day. The "eating and drinking" — "to the glory of God" — suggests a powerful sermon for contemporary Christians, but one fraught with the danger of moralism or law, not gospel, orientation.

Mark 1:40-45

This is the lovely story of the way things should be for those who really believe that Jesus is Lord. Those who are desperately ill, or in any other impossible situation, ought to be able to speak to him in prayer, ask him for healing — in true faith — and hear his response: "I will; be clean (or healed)." That's what happened in this familiar incident. A leper broke the Levitical law, approached Jesus, and instead of shouting "unclean," he begged Jesus on his knees, "If you will, you can make me clean." Jesus simply said, "I will; be clean," and the man was cured of his infirmity. Jesus told him two things: He was not to tell anyone about this healing, and, second, he was to go to the priests for re-diagnosis and a clean bill of health. The man did neither; he disobeyed Jesus and went off telling everyone what Jesus had done for him, so that Jesus was besieged by people seeking cures and healing from conditions beyond themselves, the priests, or physicians of the time. Christ intends only good health and happiness for all people.

A Sermon on the Gospel, Mark 1:40-45 — "The 'Instant' Evangelist."

A couple of decades ago, I met and lived with a black Baptist pastor for ten days; his name was Al Robb. He was a natural evangelist, who engaged everyone he met in conversations about the faith. He could talk to anybody about the things the Lord had done for him — and he did. It seemed to me that his relationship with the Lord was so intimate and genuine, and that he was so grateful for the blessings he had received from God in Jesus Christ, that he just *had* to tell people about his Lord.

I believe it was that way with the leper, who went to Jesus and was healed. I don't think he even heard what Jesus said to him — that he was so full of gratitude for his cure that he simply had to go out and tell everyone he encountered about the mercy and power he received from Jesus Christ. The man was an "instant evangelist" — no training, not even a directive — in fact, he had been forbidden — to speak about Jesus. He's something of a model, isn't he, for all who have been cleansed by Jesus in baptism and given the promise of eternal life.

1. Those who know that they have been cleansed of their sin by the Word and water of baptism are candidates for evangelism. People saved by the grace of God, and not by any good works they have done, tell others — out of gratitude — what God has done for them. That's "natural" evangelism.

2. Telling others about Jesus — basic evangelism — is equally as important as developing a spiritual life, because it is at the heart of one's response to God's grace in Jesus Christ. Like the leper, we have been healed by a word, the Word. The church needs always natural evangelists to communicate the Good News to the world.

3. Trust the Lord — and tell the world the story of how Jesus has come into your life. Become an instant evangelist, energized by the Good News in Jesus and saved by his grace.

4. The Lord in heaven blesses his evangelists, because they have taken up his work where he left off.

A Sermon on the First Lesson, 2 Kings 5:1-14 (L, C); 5:1-15 (E) and Leviticus 13:1-2, 44-46 (R) — "The Healing Word."

(Note: If I were preaching a series on these "Great Stories of the Faith," I would combine the two Old Testament readings into a single sermon, as below. However, it is more likely that I would preach on the Gospel and use the Elisha-Naaman story as an illustration.)

1. Naaman might as well have had "AIDS." There was no known cure for his leprosy, despite the fact that he was a "mighty man" in Syria's army. He was doomed to a miserable death.

2. Wasn't he lucky that he was a Syrian and not a Jew; he would have been stripped of his military position and honors and doomed to a life of social exile. (Here's where Leviticus 13 comes into the picture.)

3. It was more fortuitous that he knew a Jewess; a slave girl referred him to Elisha, and after a complicated diplomatic process he went to Elisha — and, ultimately, was cured of his leprosy. He had to humble himself before he was healed — and obey the prophet.

4. Elisha cured the man with a word, much as Jesus cleansed the leper in today's Gospel, and also as Jesus heals and restores us to a right relationship with God. The very power of God works through his Word — and gives new life to humble believers.

A Sermon on the Second Lesson, 1 Corinthians 9:24-27 (E, L, C) — "The Race of Races."

1. That's how Paul pictures the Christian life. Believers "run the course" to gain an "incorruptible crown" — eternal life, which is really a free gift of God in Christ. Running the race is living the Christian life, living out the faith.

2. Reject the rat race of the world — that is, allow the faith to determine how you live rather than permitting the world to set the agenda for your life.

3. But the spiritual life also must be developed by those who hope to finish the race. Spiritual steroids — deceiving one's self that one's good works gain God's grace, and that a person does not need to respond to the Word — will do the "runner" no good. Faith alone, through grace, prepares people for the crown.

4. Run "the race of races" to receive the crown that Jesus has already prepared for all who believe in him.

1 Corinthians 10:31—11:1 (R) — "In Imitation of Christ."

1. True believers, with Paul, attempt to live for others in imitation of Christ, which is a proper response to the Gospel of our Lord.

2. True believers will reject the "imitation life" — that is, what the world claims is "real life," living for self and what one can "get out of life."

3. True believers do those things that are pleasing to God and avoid those things which might destroy the faith that other people have in God.

4. True believers live in the shadow of the cross — and that guarantees that they will be living "in imitation of Christ."

The Transfiguration of Our Lord
Seventh Sunday after the Epiphany
Seventh Sunday in Ordinary Time

Episcopal	1 Kings 19:9-18	2 Peter 1:16-19 (20-21)	Mark 9:2-9
Lutheran	2 Kings 2:1-12a	2 Corinthians 3:12—4:2	Mark 9:2-9
Common	2 Kings 2:1-12a	2 Corinthians 4:3-6	Mark 9:2-9

(Note: The Episcopal lectionary appoints the Mark 9:2-9 Gospel, the Transfiguration story, for the last Sunday after the Epiphany, but it celebrates the Transfiguration of our Lord on the traditional date, August 6th. The Lutheran Church observes the Transfiguration on the last Sunday after Epiphany, but the Transfiguration may also be observed on August 6th. Conceivably, a Lutheran congregation might commemorate the event twice in one year. The Roman Catholic Church assigns the Transfiguration to the Second Sunday in Lent in the *Ordo*, just as it did in the old lectionary. August 6th remains the "official" feast day for the Transfiguration of our Lord. The churches using the Episcopal, Lutheran, and Common lectionaries read the Transfiguration lections on the last Sunday after the Epiphany.)

The church year theological clue:

Prior to the adoption of the new lectionary and somewhat revised church year, the Lutheran Church followed the same practice of the Episcopal Church. The propers for the Transfiguration were appointed for the last Sunday after the Epiphany, unless there was only one Sunday after the Epiphany. (With the elimination of the three "gesima" Sundays from the calendar, and the subsequent lengthening of the Epiphany season, this cannot happen anymore. There will always be at least four Sundays after the Epiphany.) The propers for the Transfiguration of Our Lord bring the Epiphany season to a fitting conclusion, while sounding a "divine echo" to the words of God that were spoken at Jesus' baptism, "You are my beloved Son, with whom I am well-pleased." In Mark, the Lord God speaks to the disciples — and in the Gospel, ultimately to the whole world — before Jesus' Passion and death: "This is my beloved son; listen to him." Hence, the Epiphany season does not simply fade away, but it ends on a genuine manifestation theme. In the perspective of Jesus' command to the disciples to keep the Transfiguration secret "until the Son of man would have risen from the dead," it also builds a liturgical and theological bridge between Epiphany and Ash Wednesday as the beginning of the Easter Cycle.

The readings:

1 Kings 19:9-18 (E)

The Roman Catholic and Lutheran churches employed this passage as the first reading for the Nineteenth Sunday of the Year (R) and the Twelfth Sunday after Pentecost of Cycle/Year A. Commentary and sermon suggestions may be found in the *Lectionary Preaching Workbook, Cycle A.*

2 Kings 2:1-12a (L)

This story of Elijah's "assumption," which occurs at the end of this pericope, was appointed for the Transfiguration because it "connects" with the appearance of Elijah and Moses "talking with Jesus" on the mountain. It has an "epiphany" quality to it, because Elisha actually sees Elijah being taken up into heaven, after the two of them have crossed the Jordan. Three times on the journey from Jerusalem to the spot of the "assumption," Elijah said to Elisha, "Tarry here, I pray you; for the Lord has sent me as far as Bethel . . . . as far as Jericho . . . . as far as the Jordan." And Elisha responded with, "As the

Lord lives, and as yourself live, I will not leave you" — on all three occasions. At the first two destinations, prophets met them and spoke to Elisha, asking him if he knew that Elijah would be taken away from him that day. He did, and at both locations he had responded, "Yes, I know; hold your peace." Elisha actually saw the chariots of fire and horses from heaven and the whirlwind, which swept Elijah up and escorted him to the realm of God — and he received a "double share of (the) spirit" of Elijah, and immediately he began doing mighty deeds in the name of God.

2 Peter 1:16-19 (20-21) (E)

This well-known assertion that the story of Jesus' Transfiguration was not fiction, nor a figment of the three disciples' imaginations, is claimed to be Peter's account of what happened on the mountain. He says, "We were eye-witnesses of his majesty," and that he and James and John actually heard the voice of God declare,"This is my beloved Son, with whom I am well pleased" (echoing Matthew's account, but omitting the "listen to him" commandment in all three evangelists' stories). Peter herein states unequivocally that the Transfiguration actually occurred. He knows it because, as with Elisha when Elijah was taken to heaven, *he was there and witnessed it.*

2 Corinthians 3:12—4:2 (L)

When Moses came down from Mount Sinai with the two stone tablets of the law, after he had been in the presence of God, "the skin on his face shone because he had been talking with God." The "glow" on his face was so great that Aaron and the rest of the people were afraid to go near him. *He had to put a veil over his face.* Paul contends (figuratively) that the veil was never removed (Did it become the veil before the Holy of Holies in the temple?), and that the Israelites were cut off from the full revelation of God. They had to wait until the coming of Christ to the world when the full glory of the lord would be revealed to all people. That glory was first seen on the mountain top, when Jesus was transfigured before Peter, James, and John. They saw God in Jesus Christ with the veil taken away. Paul would contend that there was the beginning of a change in the three disciples after that experience; they would never be the same again. God, through the Word, alters the egos, personalities, and lives of those who believe that Jesus really is the Son of God. For that reason, Paul is able to carry on his ministry in all honesty and fidelity.

Mark 9:2-9 (E, L, C)

Peter, James, and John were not present when Jesus was baptized by John the Baptizer in the Jordan, *when God spoke directly to Jesus, "you are my beloved Son, with whom I am well pleased."* The Transfiguration was a repeat performance of the conclusion of Jesus' baptism that seemed to be put on at least, even particularly, for the benefit of the three disciples. This time, as Jesus' face (in Mark's account) was made to shine like the sun itself, God came in a cloud and spoke directly to the disciples, *"This is my beloved Son."*

A week before this mountain-top experience, Jesus had been identified by Peter as the Messiah; now God himself was confirming that belief which all of the disciples shared to some extent. God did this on purpose. They needed to understand that Jesus had to die (Luke 9:31 mentions that Moses and Elijah were talking to Jesus about his coming exodus and death at Jerusalem) to complete his mission — and to be raised on the third day. So the first thing that Mark records about Jesus' instructions to the three was that "as they were coming down the mountain, he charged them to tell no one what they had seen, until the Son of man should have risen from the dead." The succeeding verses reveal that this completely puzzled them, and that they discussed it among themselves, attempting to understand what Jesus meant.

A Sermon on the Gospel, Mark 9:2-9 — "A Vision and Voice."

Years ago, when *Jesus Christ Superstar* was running on Broadway, *Time* magazine pictured the Christ as he appeared in the musical drama. He was glorified "high and lifted up" so that all could see, as though the people were on the mountain top with Peter, James, and John when Jesus was transfigured. To accomplish their purpose, the producers had to build a special apparatus, a mechanical marvel that is reminiscent of something that Leonardo da Vinci might have created. Christ was more resplendent in his gleaming, golden robe then he was in Mark's description of ultra-white clothing. He could have been either the transfigured Christ of the mountain or the risen Lord who came forth from the tomb — but, in either case, he was glorious and lifted up for all the world to see.

1. *A vision.* Christ as the Son of God is what the three disciples saw on the mountain. That vision is shared with us in the story told by Mark, informing us that in Jesus Christ the world has seen God himself.

2. *A voice.* God himself spoke to the disciples and made it manifestly clear to them that Jesus is the Son of God.

3. *A victor.* Christ could conquer sin and death, accomplishing the will of God and saving us from separation from God in the process.

Note: In preaching on this text in conjunction with 2 Corinthians 3:12—4:2, it might be a good strategy to work in Paul's contention that the *veil*, which covered Moses' face and hid the glory of the Lord, is ripped away, allowing people to see God in Jesus. The sermon would look like this:
   1. The vision.
   2. The veil.
   3. The voice.
   4. The victim.
   5. The victor.

A Sermon on the First Lesson, 2 Kings 2:1-12a (L, C) — "Elijah's Vision."

1. *A death march.* This was quite different from the death marches that occurred, for instance, in the Philippines in World War II, or the death marches of millions of refugees all over the world since then. Elijah was marching to keep an appointment with God in death, but he did not die on the way as so many other people have.

2. *A fiery chariot.* Elisha saw the "sweet chariot" and "horses of fire" actually "swing low" and separate the two of them. That was how God intervened and made his intentions known for the two prophets — one was to die, but the other was to live. Death and life were separated then and there.

3. *A heavenly vision.* It seemed to Elisha, that in his vision, Elijah was taken up by a whirlwind and transported to heaven itself. The vision meant that he knew without any doubt that God was alive and well, and that he had nothing to fear in life and death. He had actually seen a vision that would help prepare the way for Jesus' death, resurrection and ascension.

4. *A prophet's testimony.* Elijah may have been talking with Jesus about his experience with death, encouraging the Christ, along with Moses, as he faced the cross and the tomb. He, in turn, is our comfort and our hope, especially in times of suffering and death.

A Sermon on the Second Lesson, 2 Corinthians 3:12—4:2 (L) — "The Unveiling of God."

Mark reports that at Jesus' crucifixion "the veil of the Temple was torn in two from top to bottom" when Jesus died. James Stuart Stewart preached a well-known sermon on this text (Mark 15:38), in which he declared that: 1.) the rending of the veil meant "the revealing of a secret; the heart of God was laid bare;" 2.) it also testified to "the opening of a right of way (to God)" for all people; and 3.) it signified "the confirming of a hope" — the hope that death would be swallowed up in life. Paul talks about "the removal of the veil from the face of Moses, so that through Jesus Christ the glory of the Lord might shine forth into the world. Not Moses, but *God himself was unveiled when Jesus was transfigured on the mountain* (either Mount Tabor or more likely, Mount Hermon, according to many scholars).

1. Moses' face glowed with the glory of God when he returned from his encounter on Mount Sinai. It was too much for the people.Moses had to put a veil over his face, because the reflection lasted for a long time.

2. When Jesus was transfigured, God's glory was unveiled for the disciples — and for all people of faith — to see. God wants all the world to see him in Jesus Christ. God's veil is removed when people repent of their sins and turn to the Lord.

3. The "unveiled God" in Jesus Christ has the power to transform people in his own image — and he does just that.

4. Changed people — God's people — will witness most effectively in the world that Jesus is Lord, now and forever.

2 Corinthians 4:3-6 (C) — "The Glorious Face of Christ."

(Note: This reading begins where the the above lection leaves off, and it continues with the accusation in 3:15-16: "Yes, to this day whenever Moses is read a veil lies over their minds; but when a man turns to the Lord the veil is removed." Paul declares that the same thing happens when the Gospel is proclaimed to people. Unrepentant sinners, whose attention and energy are directed toward the world, hear a "veiled" Gospel which cannot create faith and new life. They cannot see the glory — the very light of God that Jesus brings into the world — in the Lord's face. But those who respond to God's call and turn to him in repentance and faith reside in that light and know the glory in the face of Jesus.

1. The Gospel of the Lord reflects the very light of God — the light that shone in Jesus' face on the mountain — into the darkness of the world to give life and hope to the people of God.

2. That some don't see the light — or the glory of God in the face of Christ — is only too obvious. Too many of us live according to Robert Louis Stevenson's dictum, "The world is so full of a number of things, I'm sure we should all be as happy as kings." Our backs are turned away from God; we can't see the glory of Jesus Christ.

3. But the light continues to shine in the darkness of this world — and the glory of the Lord, who is high and lifted up, touches our hearts and penetrates to the deepest part of our souls to light up the spiritual blindness that prevents us from responding to God. The suffering and pain on Jesus' face when he died on the cross bring us to our knees in genuine repentance.

4. Truly, it is in the Gospel of Jesus, crucified and risen Lord, that the glory that was on Jesus' face on the mountain shines into the world today. Hear the Gospel, see the glory, and God will lift you up from your knees so that you may live in light of God forever.

2 Peter 1:16-19 (E)

A sermon on this text, "We Were There," appears in the material for the Transfiguration of Our Lord in the *Lectionary Preaching Workbook, Cycle A.*

The Easter Cycle

((Note: Inasmuch as the church year remains the same from year to year, while the readings change, these comments apply to all three years/cycles of the church year. The Gospel does not alter the church year, but the church year determines how the selections of the Gospel of the Year, which is always the main reading, will be made. Most of the following material was included in the *Lectionary Preaching Workbook Cycle A*. Some revisions were necessary.)

This cycle is known as the *Easter Cycle*. It is made up of two seasons, Lent and Easter, which together form exactly one-quarter of the calendar and church year. The cycle is always thirteen weeks long, having six-and-a-half weeks in Lent and seven weeks in the Easter Season. Unlike Advent, which could exist on its own as an eschatological season, Lent cannot be separated from Easter. Lent is not, and never can be, an independent season; it has no reason for existence apart from Easter. The crucifixion of Christ is the conclusion of Lent. Without the resurrection of the Lord, Jesus would only be a martyr, or worse, and the human race would still be mired down in sin. Easter is the heart of the entire church year and of the Gospel as well. Since Easter — the great fifty days — is the "essential season" of the church year, it gives its name to the entire cycle.

Easter, of course, deals with the redeeming events, the death and resurrection of the Lord. It puts its mark on every Sunday of the year; every Sunday is a "little Easter," a celebration of the cross and the tomb. In this respect, Easter is a unitive event, always keeping death and resurrection together. But there are practical problems, both in worship and preaching, and one of these problems is that church people don't have a very good grasp of the nature of the Easter cycle and the manner in which Lent and Easter are inextricably bound together. Lent is probably the more popular season, according to attendance during the forty days of Lent. Just when the impact of the resurrection should swell the cry of the church, "Christ is risen! He is risen, indeed!", the zeal of the people begins to flag and participation in worship (and maybe work too) lessens. It is important for pastors to keep the two seasons together in their homiletical planning and their preaching. Practically, Lent has almost supplanted Easter as the essential season of the church year; it represents, as celebrated in most churches, a reversal of the practices and the anastasial theology of the early Church.

The Season of Lent

Lent is a period of forty days, penitential in nature, and taking its shape from the forty days that Jesus spent in the desert after his baptism in the Jordan. It has biblical connections with the forty days Moses spent on Mount Sinai and Elijah's forty-day journey to Mount Horeb (both of which were also fasts). Actually, Lent assumed its shape and length gradually in something of an evolutionary process. At first, it was only a three-day observance. Later it took the shape of a three-week period, and then later had different lengths in various parts of the church until finally it became the six-and-a-half week season (nine-and-a-half weeks before the pre-Lent — the "gesima" Sundays — were taken from Lent) that it is today.

Lent apparently did not take the shape of a long preparatory fast until it was expanded from the *triduum* (Good Friday, Holy Saturday, and Easter) to three weeks and then to forty days. Sundays were not part of the Lenten fast. *At first, that fast began on what is now the First Sunday in Lent — originally known as the* quadrigesima, *or forty days before Easter (before the* triduum*). That is why the First Sunday in Lent always uses the gospel reading that tells the story of Jesus' forty days in the desert wilderness. The model for Lent is found in this forty-day fast.* Later, Sundays were removed from Lent and the extra days, Ash Wednesday to the Saturday before the First Sunday of Lent, were added. In some places, the *triduum* now became Holy Thursday, Good Friday, and Holy Saturday. *Later, the pre-Lent Sundays were added — the* quinquagesima, *then* sexagesima, *and, finally,* septuagesima, *as fifty, sixty, and seventy days before Easter.*

The primary reason for lengthening Lent had to do with the final period of preparation for the catechumens of the early church who were to be baptized on Easter Sunday. As Lent became longer and the faithful joined the catechumens in the observance of Lent, Lent lost much of its pre-confirmation character and became a season primarily devoted to spiritual preparation for Easter. It was the primary penitential season of the church year. The Lenten discipline, which was supposed to be undertaken by the faithful for the forty days of Lent, consisted primarily of *fasting, almsgiving, and prayer.* The traditional Gospel for Ash Wednesday, from Matthew 6, outlines these three-fold marks of the faithful "keeping" of Lent that all of the members of the church should make part of their daily lives. Lent took on the character of a "spring revival" in much of the church. The contemporary world situation that the church finds itself in calls for new interpretations of Lenten discipline to turn the people of God toward the suffering and desperate needs of people today and to put the human predicament before the cross of Christ. Lent cannot be an exclusively "interiorized" spiritual journey; the suffering of Christ does not allow that in light of people's problems today.

Pastors, in their preaching ministry, should remember that Lent was connected to Easter through the passion and death of the Lord *and also in the Sacrament of Baptism.* Easter was the principal day for baptism. Lent, in that time, had the character of an educational, as well as spiritual, event for the catechumens. They underwent three "scrutinies," which consisted of exorcisms and instructions in the faith They were instructed in the secrets of the church (the Creed, the Lord's Prayer, etc.). Finally, they were baptized on Easter Day. Some congregtions today are returning to the ancient practice of doing the final educational and ceremonial rites of confirmation during Lent, scheduling confirmation on the Sunday of the Passion, if it can't be scheduled for Easter Sunday. The rediscovery and reconstruction of the Easter vigil has led to the reaffirmation on the baptismal covenant of the believers in attendance at this the first eucharist of Easter. These developments suggest that the theological framework of Lent is baptismal, in which people are incorporated into the death and resurrection of Jesus Christ. In baptismal preaching, the pastor may discover the best way to make the most of Lent and also of the entire Easter Cycle. For examples of such preaching, see my *Plastic Flowers in the Holy Water* (C.S.S.), *You Are My Beloved* (with Frederick Kemper, Concordia), and *Is the Cross Still There? Letter to Jennifer,* (C.S.S.).

The problems pastors face as they prepare their preaching for Lent may be these:

1. Lent tends to be too long for most people to sustain a penitential mood. Years ago suggestions were made proposing that Lent be reduced to two weeks (which would have been comparable to Passiontide, at the time). The Passion of the Lord actually occupies only one week of the church year today.

2. Lent tends to dominate the worship and preaching of the Easter cycle. Many pastors say that this is the only time of the year that they plan their sermons for the entire period. (Suggestion: Plan a preaching agenda for the entire Easter Cycle.)

3. Lent has almost become a "Sunday-only season" for most contemporary Christians. A few of the faithful keep the fast by attending and participating in weekday services of Lent. Preachers, therefore, have to make the most of Sunday preaching during Lent.

4. Lent has become a "bloodless sacrifice" for most, possibly because the almost-exclusive preaching emphasis on the passion and death of Christ has tended to diminish the dimensions of the human predicament, sin and death, which are responsible for so much human pain and suffering. Lent is about this human predicament — and how God deals with sin and death in Jesus Christ.

5. Lent has become so Good Friday oriented that the joy of Easter is muted and the theological dimensions of new life in Christ — through baptism, which is the point of participating in the discipline of Lent — are reduced, even lost.

6. Easter, therefore, has become a one-day celebration instead of the "essential season" of the church year.

To make the most of preaching during Lent, the pastor must understand the nature of the Easter cycle and plan the worship and preaching for the entire cycle before Lent begins from both sides of the cross and empty tomb — *and with the involvement of the faithful through the renewal of their baptismal covenant.* Over against Ash Wednesday's sobering word, "You are dust and unto dust you shall return." The Gospel promise of the risen Lord, "Behold, I make all things new," has to be sounded loudly and clearly.

In summary, it remains that Ash Wednesday — over against the Easter event (cross and resurrection) — is the liturgical, homiletical, and theological key to the worship and preaching of Lent. Its *first* word is, "Remember, you are dust, and unto dust you shall return." The Gospel for Ash Wednesday is the traditional one. (Only one set of pericopes is prescribed for all three years of the lectionary — Matthew 6:1-6, 16-21; the other readings from Joel 2 and 2 Corinthians 5 and 6 are also traditional.) The Ash Wednesday Gospel makes it perfectly clear that Lent is about the human predicament, sin and death, rather than entirely about the passion and death of Christ. Holy Week and Easter inform the church how God has dealt with human frailty and the inability of people to obey his commandments and save themselves from the Devil and death in the death and resurrection of Jesus. This predicament — sin and death — finds resolution in preaching baptism in the context of incorporation into the new covenant in Jesus and the Body of Christ, the church. Ash Wednesday's terrifying reminder is answered in baptismal preaching during Lent: *those who die with Christ in baptism also share in his resurrection and the new life of the risen Lord.*

In light of all this, planning for worship and preaching during Lent is of crucial importance. Lent is the one time of the year that parish pastors, who may exist on a kind of hand-to-mouth homiletical regimen from Sunday to Sunday, do plan in detail. *But most of us plan only for Lent and fail to plan for Easter.* I suggest that planning for the entire Easter Cycle is necessary if one is going to be faithful to the church year themes in the Sunday and weekly opportunities to proclaim the Good News to people. When congregations perceive how seriously their pastors are taking their preaching ministries during the entire Easter Cycle — and not just Lent — they will most likely respond by attending worship with more regularity and enthusiasm and may even learn to make more out of Lent and Easter, so as to live out their baptism in the world.

Ash Wednesday

(Note: There is only one set of readings and liturgical appointments for Ash Wednesday. Last year's comments apply to Year/Cycle B, and the sermon suggestions in the *Lectionary Preaching Workbook, Cycle A,* continue to have relevance. An additional sermon suggestion for the missing portion of the Ash Wednesday Gospel [Matthew 6:7-15, the Lord's Prayer] has been added, along with a Sunday series of sermons for Lent that amplifies the baptismal motif of the Easter Cycle.)

Joel 2:12-19   *2 Corinthians 5:20b—6:2*   *Matthew 6:1-6, 16-18 (19-21)*

The church year theological clue

The title of this day — Ash Wednesday (the rite when ashes are placed on the foreheads of penitents with the words, "You are dust, and unto dust you will return") — provides the theological clue for preaching during Lent and Easter. Every person who is born here on the earth will sooner or later be claimed by death. The Genesis 3 story is certainly true, in this respect: no one is exempt from death. Even Jesus, the very Son of God, had to die, partly because his incarnation caused him to share fully in the human experience of life and death, and because he was born to atone for the sins of others and bestow salvation upon repentant sinners. The grip of death is destroyed and people are released in the resurrection of Jesus Christ. Easter reverses Ash Wednesday's awful announcement and says, "You are children of God, and through the living Christ you shall live forever." The death of human beings is preached during the season of Lent in the shadow of the cross; Jesus had to die in order to conquer death once and for all. The final and total victory will come with the parousia. When Jesus returns, death, which has been already conquered by Christ, will be no more. The Second Coming of the Lord will usher in the day of abundant and eternal life for the children of God.

Lent is the season when the ashes of Death are washed away again as the baptismal covenant with God is renewed. It is the time when the people of God participate in the death and resurrection of the Lord. They realize the conquest of death by their Lord and know that victory — forgiveness and eternal life — is promised them in their baptism. Baptism has to be the heart of worship and devotions, teaching and preaching, if people are to make the most of Lent and Easter.

The Prayer of the Day (LBW)

This is simply a revision of the traditional and classic Ash Wednesday collect appointed for use in many of the Western churches. God is addressed as a creator who loves all that he has made and forgives penitent sinners for their wrong-doings. The petition for God's grace looks to the cross and the empty tomb, asking God to "create in us new and honest hearts, so that, truly repenting of our sins, we may obtain from you, the God of all mercy, full pardon and forgiveness; through your Son, Jesus Christ our Lord, who lives and reigns with you and the Holy Spirit, one God, now and forever." (In some parts of the church, this collect may be said as the first collect every day in Lent.)

The Psalm of the Day (LBW)

Psalm 51 — This is the plea of a penitent (David, it is assumed) who is deeply aware of his sin, searches his heart, and lifts up his voice to his Maker, pleading for mercy and forgiveness. It is one of the most abject prayers of confession and pardon in the whole Bible. The penitent knows the character of God, because he asks ("in your great compassion") for ultimate absolution — "Blot out my transgressions." He knows his own situation perfectly, "I know my transgressions, and my sin is ever before me," and even that "I have been wicked from my birth, a sinner from my mother's womb." The intensity — and singular beauty — of his plea heightens with these words that found their way, for obvious reasons, into the liturgies of the church long ago: "Purge me from my sin, and I shall be pure; wash me, and I shall be clean indeed [a baptismal connection] . . . . Hide your face from my sins and blot out all my iniquities . . . . Create in me a clean heart, O God, and renew a right spirit within me . . . . Cast me not away from your presence, and take not your Holy Spirit from me . . . . Give me the joy of your saving help again, and sustain me with your bountiful spirit." As the Psalmist nears the end of his prayer, he cries out the word that all who have heard God's Word in the Garden ("You are dust, and unto dust you will return") need to address God — *Deliver me from death, O God, and my tongue shall sing of your righteousness, O God of my salvation.* When he adds, "The sacrifice of God is a broken spirit, a broken and a contrite heart, O God, you will not despise," there is no mistaking that this is a psalm for Lent, especially for Ash Wednesday.

The Psalm Prayer

Almighty and merciful Father, you freely forgive those who, as David of old, acknowledge and confess their sins. Create in us pure hearts, and wash away all our sins in the blood of your dear Son, Jesus Christ our Lord. (Clearly, this, too, is not only a prayer for Ash Wednesday, but one that is also suitable for the entire season.)

The readings:

Joel 2:12-19

In this reading, it is God himself who issues the *invitation* to begin the season of Lent by engaging in the penitential discipline described in this text, which is reiterated in a different form and then expanded in Jesus' teaching in Matthew 6, the Gospel for the Day. The invitation is to "return to the lord, your God, for he is gracious and merciful, slow to anger, and abounding in steadfast love." With the invitation, there is also a *command* that is most appropriate for Ash Wednesday and the full season of Lent: "Blow the trumpet in Zion; sanctify a fast; call a solemn assembly; gather the people." Those who respond, or in the case of Christians, "keep Lent," tell the world that they know "where" their God is; he is "in Christ, reconciling the world to himself." The final part is a *promise* to the people of Israel: "The Lord had pity on his people . . . and said, . . . 'Behold, I am sending you grain, wine, and oil [the eucharist for Christians?], and you will be satisfied; *and I will no more make you a reproach among the nations'."* God is as good as his promise; the death and resurrection of our Lord tell us that.

2 Corinthians 5:20b—6:2

Paul's plea to the church at Corinth ("We beseech you on behalf of Christ, be reconciled to God.") speaks specifically of the mercy God has extended to the world to all who know themselves to be sinners. Jesus became "sin, who knew no sin, so that in him we might become the righteousness of God." This is almost an accusation toward the Corinthian congregation — which might be one of our problems, too — that they have not taken the Gospel as seriously as they should have, apparently not comprehending that their sin separates them from God when it goes unrecognized and unconfessed. Genuinely repentant sinners, who base their hope of forgiveness and new life on Christ, are the only ones who can really be reconciled to God, because reconciliation comes through Jesus' death on Golgotha. His plea ("We entreat you not to accept the grace of God in vain.") points to the root of our predicament in our separation from God, assuring us that God will accept us forever in the Lord. Lent, for the Christian, "is the acceptable time; behold, now is the day of salvation."

Matthew 6:1-6, 16-18 (19-21)

The spiritual discipline of Lent is spelled out in detail in this Gospel in the context of, as Jesus puts it, "your Father who sees in secret (and) will reward you." In the practice of "piety," Jesus lists almsgiving first and directs that it should be done secretly and without any show of generosity. To advertise one's charity, so that others may see it and praise the giver, is unacceptable to God. To those whose giving has been acknowledged by others, Jesus says, "You have already received your reward." Prayer is the second act of piety that godly persons should practice, but people dare not pray in ways that bring attention to one's religiosity; such prayer, which is done for the benefit of others and is not really directed to God, is hypocritical and, therefore, worthless. Fasting, which is the last of the three acts of piety in Jesus' teaching, and is almost unknown among Americans, is also a spiritual exercise that has no merit unless it is performed to heighten one's sense of self-denial and the quest for the presence of God. In his forty days in the wilderness, Jesus engaged in two of these disciplines and did so in a one-on-one relationship with his heavenly Father. This, no doubt, sustained him when the Tempter tried to win him over to himself. When we follow his example, these devotional actions are not only expressions of penitence and self-denial, but are also signs of our complete dependence upon Jesus Christ for salvation, who is our *treasure.* He is the one who claims our hearts for as long as we live, for he alone is our salvation. Our almsgiving, prayers, and fasting are expressions of our gratitude and love, as well as *repentance.*

(Note: One of the puzzles about this traditional Gospel is that the Lord's Prayer has been omitted from the Ash Wednesday pericope. Since Jesus gave it to the disciples to teach them how to pray, it might be used for mid-week preaching, or, in some situations that are isolated by pastoral exegesis, as a Sunday sermon series. It is this "missing piece" in the Ash Wednesday puzzle that the sermon suggestions will consider in the context of baptism for Series/Cycle B. Incidentally, a sermon series on the Lord's Prayer makes an effective sermon series for the Wednesday of Lent.)

A Sermon on the Gospel, Matthew 6:7-15 — "Forgiveness — God's Baptismal Gift."

God bestows the gift of forgiveness, which brings reconciliation with him and new life, through the sacrament of baptism. *Lent is the time we re-experience our baptism; it is a kind of annual baptism, not simply a spring revival, for the faithful.* With the first words of Ash Wednesday still ringing in our ears, we hear a word of hope and joy,

> *In holy baptism our gracious Heavenly Father liberates us from sin and death by joining us to the death and resurrection of our Lord Jesus Christ. We are born children of a fallen humanity; in the waters of baptism we are reborn children of God and inheritors of eternal life. By water and the Holy Spirit we are made members of the church which is the body of Christ. As we live with him and his people, we grow in faith, love, and obedience to the will of God.*

1. Sinners all, because we are baptized we may boldly and expectantly pray, "Forgive us our sins" — knowing that the God, who already has forgiven us in baptism, will do so again. This is the prayer of repentant sinners, who seek reconciliation with God and renewal in Jesus Christ.

2. Repentant sinners are reconcilers themselves, forgiving their enemies as God forgives them. They forgive because they have been forgiven. As Tennyson's King Arthur said to his unfaithful queen, "Lo, I forgive thee, as the eternal God forgives."

3. People who refuse to forgive others for the wrongs done to them do not qualify for receiving the forgiveness of their sins by the Father. Forgiving others for what they have done to us does not win God's forgiveness and love, but refusing to forgive one's enemies makes one ineligible for God's forgiveness; such people are really unrepentant.

4. The Ash Wednesday communion renews our baptismal covenant and the forgiveness that is ours in Christ. It, as a participation in the death and resurrection of the Lord, offers a pattern for our daily lives — dying and rising in the Lord — as well as for Lent.

A Sermon Series on Old Testament Readings for Lent

In the context of baptism, these readings reinforce the theological clue: through baptism, God claims believers as his children. (See *You Are My Beloved Children* by GMB, Concordia Publishing House. Fred Kemper wrote the first section, *You Are My Beloved Son*.)

First Sunday in Lent, Genesis 2:7-9, 15-17; 3:1-7 — "Created as Children of God."

Second Sunday in Lent, Genesis 7:1-5, 11-12, 17-23 — "New Life for the Children of God."

Third Sunday in Lent, Jonah 3:1-10 — "God Relents When His People Repent."

Fourth Sunday in Lent, Isaiah 55:1-11 — "From Fast to Feast."

Fifth Sunday in Lent — Genesis 22:1-18 — "The Incredible Sacrifice."

Sunday of the Passion, Exodus 12:1-14, 29-34 — "The Passover and the Passion."

(Note: This series also continues through Eastertide so that both Lent and Easter are baptismally oriented. Other suggestions for Lenten preaching are included in the *Lectionary Preaching Workbook, Cycle A*.)

First Sunday in Lent

Roman Catholic	**Genesis 9:8-15**	**1 Peter 3:18-22**	**Mark 1:12-15**
Episcopal	**Genesis 9:8-17**	**1 Peter 3:18-22**	**Mark 1:9-13**
Lutheran	**Genesis 22:1-18**	**Romans 8:31-39**	**Mark 1:12-15**
Common	**Genesis 9:8-17**	**1 Peter 3:18-22**	**Mark 1:9-15**

The church year theological clue

Historically, most of the liturgical churches celebrate the First Sunday in Lent as Invocabit, as the ancient introit announces: "He shall call upon me, and I will answer him. I will deliver him and honor him. With long life will I satisfy him and show him my salvation. He that dwelleth in the secret place of the most High shall abide under the shadow of the Almighty." The classic introit rearranges the verses of Psalm 91, that are used by beginning with verses 15 and 16 in the antiphon, with verse 1 as the liturgical remnant in the psalm verse. There can be little doubt that this entire psalm was once sung on this day, the *Quadragesima* — forty days before Easter and the beginning of Lent for centuries — because it declares: "He shall give his angels charge over thee, to keep thee in all thy ways. They shall bear thee up lest thou dash thy foot against a stone." (vv. 11, 12) The psalm pointedly connects the Passion of Jesus to the Resurrection of the crucified Christ, building a bridge that prevents people from celebrating Lent as a penitential season without crossing over to Easter, the season of joy and hope in the victory of Jesus Christ over death. The preacher must remember that for many people in the congregation, the First Sunday in Lent *is* the beginning of Lent. Pastors ought to also be cognizant of the fact that Lent cannot exist without Easter, and that the forty days of preparation need the balance of the Great Fifty Days of Easter.

The Prayer of the Day

The classic collect called upon God to "stretch forth the right hand of thy Majesty to defend us from them that rise up against us," thereby applying the temptation of Jesus to the human situation, especially in Lent. Contemporary prayers sound a similar note, as in the Episcopal *Book of Common Prayer*: "Come quickly to help us who are assaulted by many temptations; and, as you know the weaknesses of each of us, let each one find you mighty to save." The first of two prayers in the *Lutheran Book of Worship* gives Lent an "exodus" character that is, at once, both existential and eschatological: "Guide the people of your church, that following our Savior, we may walk through the wilderness of this world toward the glory of the world to come." The second prayer, which has baptismal undertones in it, with a suggestion of dying and rising daily in repentance, gives topological treatment to the Gospel for the Day: "Lord God, our strength, the battle of good and evil rages within and around us, and our ancient foe tempts us with his deceits and empty promises. Keep us steadfast in your Word and, when we fall, raise us again and restore us through your Son, Jesus Christ our Lord . . . ." Christ's "temptation in the wilderness" is a story that we know well, but there is a difference; Jesus overcame temptation set before him by Satan, but we — more often than not — fall and need to repent of our sin. Lent gives us that chance.

The Psalm of the Day

Psalm 25, or 25:3-9 (E); 25:4-9 (R) — The Episcopal and Roman Catholic churches give multiple liturgical assignments to this psalm. Both use it in Series/Cycle A (Twenty-sixth Sunday of the Year [R]; Proper Twenty-one [E]), as well as on this First Sunday in Lent. The Roman Catholic Church also employs it on the Third Sunday of the Year (B), and on the First Sunday of Advent (C). That it is a popular liturgical song is evident, but it is especially appropriate for Lent: "Show me your ways, O Lord, and teach me your paths (E).

Lead me in your truth and teach me, for you are the God of my salvation; in you have I trusted all the day long.'' (E, R) The psalm not only accommodates the liturgy and theology of Lent, but it also, as used here, harks back to the time when God made his covenant with his people. In this larger setting, the people of God ask in repentance for the forgiveness of God for their transgressions and deliverance into new life.

(Note: The LBW appoints this psalm to three Sundays: The Nineteenth Sunday after Pentecost [A]; the First Sunday of Advent [C]; and the Eighth Sunday after Pentecost [C].)

Psalm 6 (L) — The penitential theme in this psalm, which is coupled with the knowledge of God's graciousness and love that issue forth in forgiveness, offers a reason for its selection for this Sunday's liturgy. It sets forth the human condition: ''Have pity on me, O Lord, for I am weak; heal me, for my bones are wracked . . . . Turn, O Lord, and deliver me; save me for your mercy's sake.'' It is, at once, a call to repentance during Lent, which comes to a halt before the cross: ''For in death no one remembers you; and who will give thanks in the grave?'' The psalmist banishes — as Jesus did Satan — those who tempt him (the ''evildoers''), and reflects the real joy that comes only with the resurrection (v. 9): ''The Lord has heard my supplication; the Lord accepts my prayer.''

The Psalm Prayer (LBW)

Lord God, you love mercy and tenderness; you give life and overcome death. Look upon the weakness and grief of your church; restore it to health by your risen Son, so that it may sing a new song in your praise; through your Son, Jesus Christ our Lord.

The readings:

Genesis 9:8-15 (R); 9:8-17 (E, C)

This post-flood story — in which God establishes an everlasting covenant between himself, Noah, and all people, declaring that he will never again cause a flood to wipe out all life on earth — has been selected, partly, because it depicts God's intention to redeem his people, rather than destroy them. Along with the new covenant, God, as he always does, provides a sign — the rainbow — as a token of his fidelity to his covenant. But the reading was chosen for at least one other reason: it is a type of baptism. The ''flood waters'' of baptism wash away the sins of God's people and, in the process, restore them to communion with God. Luther's magnificent ''flood prayer'' for baptism, which has been revised in the LBW, declares:

By the waters of the flood you condemned the wicked and saved those whom you had chosen, Noah and his family . . . . By the baptism of his own death and resurrection your beloved Son has set us free from the bondage to sin and death, and has opened the way to the joy and freedom of everlasting life. He made water a sign of the kingdom and of cleansing and rebirth . . . . Pour out your Holy Spirit, so that those who are here baptized may be given new life. Wash away the sin of all those who are cleansed by this water and bring them forth as inheritors of your glorious kingdom.

Genesis 22:1-18 (L)

In this familiar story, Abraham hears the voice of God, answers him and learns that God wants him to offer his son, Isaac, as a sacrifice to prove his faith in the Lord God. Abraham does as he is commanded, taking Isaac and two servants on a three-day journey to a place in the land of Moriah indicated by God. There an altar was built, wood collected for the fire, and the boy bound and placed on the altar. As the story goes, God intervened when

Abraham raised his knife and commended Abraham for his faith — "God himself will provide the sacrifice." God did just that; a ram was found with its horns ensnared in a bush and it became the burnt offering. The story accommodates the Lutheran emphasis, in the lectionary during Lent, on the passion and death of Jesus, rather than on the predicament of humanity and the deliverance that baptism provides. It is, of course, a type of the loving sacrifice of the only begotten Son (John 3:16) on the cross.

1 Peter 3:18-22 (R, E, C)

Variations of this pericope were assigned to the Sixth Sunday of Easter, Series/Cycle A in several lectionaries (1 Peter 3:15-18 [R]; 3:8-18 [E]; 3:15-22 [L]; 3:13-22 [C]). Interestingly, three of the four lectionaries assign exactly the same verses of 1 Peter 3 to this Sunday in Year B. The reason is simply that, if 1 Peter is accepted as a baptismal homily, this passage complements the baptismal typology of Genesis 9 and the baptismal content of Lent. Comments on this text are included in the material for the Sixth Sunday of Easter, Cycle/Series A, *Lectionary Preaching Workbook.*

Romans 8:31-39 (L)

Selections from Romans comprise the first readings for the first three Sundays in Lent, possibly to pick up portions of Romans not read in the Pentecost season, Series/Cycle A. (Part of Romans 5 is assigned to the Fourth Sunday after Pentecost; verses 31-34 of Chapter 8 are omitted from the readings on the Tenth and Eleventh Sundays after Pentecost, but not in Lent. Four of the first readings in Lent, Series/Cycle A, are also from Romans.) Those who have attended many Christian funeral services will be familiar with this magnificent statement of faith in the crucified and risen Lord: "If God is for us, who is against us? He who did not spare his own Son but gave him up for us all, will he not also give us all things with him? . . . [nothing] will be able to separate us from the love of God in Christ Jesus our Lord." This reading, with its "He who did not spare his own Son but gave him up for us all," complements the theme of Genesis 22, carrying it to the ultimate climax of Jesus' death at Calvary. This text highlights what God's gift in Jesus accomplishes for people of faith.

Mark 1:9-13 (E); 1:9-15 (C); 1:12-15 (R, L)

Mark's version of Jesus' temptation is so brief that one could get the impression that he considered the incident to be of little or no importance. He has the basic ingredients of Matthew's and Luke's stories — the forty days, Satan, wild beasts, and angels — but the temptation itself is not detailed. After his baptism, Mark tells us, "The Spirit immediately drove him [Jesus] out into the wilderness," therein making a closer connection between Jesus' baptism and temptation than the other two writers. Instead, he prepares a neat little package to get his point across. Jesus, whom God identified as his "beloved Son" at his baptism, overcame Satan, was not harmed by the wild beasts, and was "ministered" to ("fed") by the very angels of God. Unlike the first Adam, who could not stand firm against the wiles of Satan, Jesus proved to Satan — and the world — that the Evil One had met his match. Jesus, the new Adam, was the victor, and Satan was defeated once and for all.

A Sermon on the Gospel, Mark 1:9-13 (E); 1:9-15 (C); 1:12-15 (R, L) — "Satan Meets His Match."

When they moved into our neighborhood, the young couple and their two children seemed to be an ideal family. They were intelligent — he was a professor and a Ph.D. — personable, and affable. They were a splendid addition to the families living on the street; they responded to their welcome party with an open house for the neighbors, and entered into the various activities that went on in the neighborhood. The man and woman seemed to be a very loving couple, who nurtured their sons very carefully. They saw to it that each of the sons returned to his native country in Europe for catechetical instruction and confirmation. They seemed to have an extremely high level of values. But after they had lived in the neighborhood several years something happened and the family nearly disintegrated. The husband/father fell in love with a young woman who worked for him. When his wife found out about the affair, she confronted him with her knowledge. He did not deny it and offered a weak excuse, ''I couldn't help myself. I can't help myself now.'' His wife, when asked why she put up with his infidelity, replied, ''I love him too much to divorce him.'' Her love ultimately won out and saved the marriage and preserved their family when it might have been smashed to pieces.

1. *Jesus could — and did — help himself when Satan tempted him. He simply said ''no'' to Satan and defeated him.* He acted as the faithful Son of God, and out of love accomplished for us what we would have never been able to do by ourselves.

2. *Jesus showed us that to be obedient to God — that is, to say ''Yes'' to God — means that we must say ''No'' to Satan.* God expects us to be his obedient people, as a consequence of our baptism. God gives us the ability to say ''yes'' or ''no'' to temptation; he gave us the freedom to make choices between good and evil for ourselves.

3. *There are situations in which we can — and should — say ''No'' to Satan.* Through the help of Christ we can overcome temptation. Such victories are his, not merely ours. He helps us when we can't seem to help ourselves.

4. *Satan wins too many of the battles we find ourselves in.* But even when we triumph, the victory does not win forgiveness and eternal life for us; Jesus has done that for us in the wilderness and at the Tree of Golgotha.

A Sermon on the First Lesson, Genesis 9:8-15 (R); 9:8-17 (E, C) — ''The Cross Holds Up the Rainbow.''

The earth, God's garden, has been a graveyard twice in the history of humanity, according to the Bible. Today we live in the fear that it may soon be a graveyard for a third time — and forever!

When Noah survived the Flood, spending over a year cooped up in that ark, he set foot into a graveyard, for no forms of life survived on land with the exception of the creatures on that ship. The bones of the corpses claimed by the Flood had been covered up by the shifting sands and soil. The earth was washed clean; it was a garden again, much like the beginning of creation. An eerie silence must have greeted the first beings to disembark from that boat; only the sounds of the animals who still lived could be heard. Echoes were everywhere. But Noah built an altar, offered sacrifices of thanksgiving to God, and got an answer: ''I will never again curse the ground with a flood . . . I establish my covenant between you and your descendants after you . . . I set my bow in the cloud, and it shall be a sign of my covenant.''

1. *It is God's intention to preserve people and the earth, not destroy it.* The covenant he made with Noah affirms this; the rainbow announces and reannounces the covenant.

2. *Human beings seem to be intent on destroying the earth and themselves, in the process.* Acid rain and pollution, depletion of natural resources, and nuclear fallout threaten to destroy the earth and all life. But the rainbow still arches above the earth after a storm! (Loren Eiseley's parable of the ''Star Thrower,'' which is printed in *The Unexpected Universe* and *The Star Thrower,* speaks of this predicament.)

3. *The Cross holds up the rainbow.* The death of Jesus — the cross — is the eternal sign of God's concern for human beings and a statement that he has not given up on the human race. Cross and rainbow combine as a sign of hope. The faithful in Christ will do what they have to do to hold up the cross by learning to care for the earth and all life.

4. *Through his life and death, Jesus changed the graveyard into a garden.* He draws us to himself and his cross so that with and through us he might do it again!

A Sermon on the Second Lesson, 1 Peter 3:18-22

See the "Dancing Waters" sermon in the *Lectionary Preaching Workbook, Cycle A,* for the Sixth Sunday of Easter. It is a baptismal sermon, appropriate for either Lent or Easter.

Romans 8:31-39

See the sermon "Questions and Answers of the Faith" in the *Lectionary Preaching Workbook, Cycle A.*

Second Sunday in Lent

Roman Catholic	**Genesis 22:1-2, 9-13, 15-18**	**Romans 8:31-34**	**Mark 9:2-10**
Episcopal	**Genesis 22:1-14**	**Romans 8:31-39**	**Mark 8:31-38**
Lutheran	**Genesis 28:10-17 (18-22)**	**Romans 5:1-11**	**Mark 8:31-38**
Common	**Genesis 17:1-10, 15-19**	**Romans 4:16-25**	**Mark 8:31-38**

The church year theological clue

The Sunday received its title — *Reminiscere* — from verse 5 of the Twenty-fifth Psalm, "Remember, O Lord, your compassion and love, for they are from everlasting." This is meant to be a kind of "remembrance Sunday" — as all Sundays are, recalling the death and resurrection of our Lord as "little Easters" — but with a difference. The church is being asked to remember the identity of Jesus Christ as the Son of God, and that the passion and death of the Lord are fairly close at hand. Jesus was the One *par excellence* who could say, "To you, O Lord, I lift up my soul; my God, I put my trust in you; let me not be humiliated, nor let my enemies triumph over me." And the faithful, as baptized members of the Body of Christ, are to remember their sinful estate and turn to God in repentance and faith this day and every day. The Sunday — *Remembrance Sunday* — is a model for the faith and life of the Christian.

The Prayer of the Day

The traditional collect for this Sunday speaks to the human condition and what Luther would have called "the bondage of the will." The Episcopal prayer for this Sunday strikes the note common to most contemporary "remembrance" collects:

> *O God, whose glory it is always to have mercy: Be gracious to all who have gone astray from your ways, and bring them again with penitent hearts and steadfast faith to embrace and hold fast the unchangeable truth of your Word, Jesus Christ your Son; who with you and the Holy Spirit lives and reigns, one God for ever and ever.*

The LBW contains two prayers for this day; the first is quite similar to the *Book of Common Prayer* collect, while the second was written to complement the John 4 Gospel in Series/Cycle A.

The Psalm of the Day

Psalm 16, or 16:5-11 (E) — This is a psalm that speaks to the passion of the Lord:

> *Protect me, O God, for I take refuge in you; I have said to the Lord, "You are my Lord, my God above all other"* . . . *I have set the Lord always before me; because he is at my right hand I shall not fall. My heart, therefore, is glad, and my spirit rejoices.* My body also shall rest in hope. For you will not abandon me to the grave, nor let your holy one see the pit . . . You will show me the path of life. (emphasis mine)

It picks up and highlights the emphasis on Jesus' impending suffering and death in the Mark 8 Gospel, and the "remembrance" theme of the day.

Psalm 115:1, 9-18 (L) — Put into the context of this day, this could be the cry of a person who remembers the goodness — the love and faithfulness — of God and his deliverance from an impossible situation, even sin and death. Because this individual remembers the mercies of God, he/she turns to the Lord and praises him for the gracious gifts of God that have been received. Those who remember the mercies of the Lord God in Jesus Christ ought to, spontaneously, "bless the Lord, from this time forth for evermore. Hallelujah."

Psalm 116:10, 15-19 (R) — The predicament that Abraham and Isaac found themselves in had to be in mind of the people who selected this psalm for Remembrance Sunday. The words of the psalm could have been spoken by Isaac:

> *I love the Lord, because he has heard the voice of my supplication . . . . The cords of death entangled me; the grip of the grave took hold of me; I came to grief and sorrow . . . . Turn again to your rest, O my soul, for the Lord has treated you well.* For you have rescued my life from death, my eyes from tears, and my feet from stumbling. I will walk in the presence of the Lord in the land of the living. (emphasis mine)

A theologically informed and faithful Christian might say the same thing.

The Psalm Prayer — Psalm 116 (LBW)

> *God of power and mercy, through the Passion and resurrection of your Son you have freed us from the bonds of death and the anguish of separation from you. Be with us on our pilgrimage, and help us offer you a sacrifice of praise, fulfill our vows, and glorify you in the presence of all your people; through Jesus Christ our Lord.*

The readings:

Genesis 22:1-2, 9-13, 15-18 (R); 22:1-14 (E)

The Lutheran lectionary appointed this reading for last Sunday, the First Sunday in Lent, Series/Cycle B. Commentary may be found there.

Genesis 17:1-10, 15-19 (C)

The story of God's visit to Abram, when he was ninety-nine years old, begins with a change in name from Abram to Abraham, and the promise of an "everlasting covenant" between God and Abraham and his offspring. God also changes the name of Abraham's wife from Sarai to Sarah, but God made Abraham laugh when he declared that he and Sarah would have a son, who would be named Isaac. Abraham was virtually 100 years old and Sarah was ninety when God informed them of the impending birth of a special child, who would be the inheritor of the covenant the Lord made with Abraham. This is one of the great stories of faith, which needs to be remembered, particularly in the perspective of the new covenant God made with the world in Jesus Christ.

Genesis 28:10-17 (18-22) (L)

There seems to be virtually no connection between this reading, which is another great story of faith, and the Gospel for the Day (Mark 8:31-38). It would actually complement the Roman Catholic choice of Mark 9:2-10, the Transfiguration story, much better than Mark 8. The family story of Jacob's dream, as he camped out at night on the journey from Beersheba to Haran, tells about the ladder from earth to heaven with angels ascending and descending it — and God's promise to keep and bless Jacob wherever he went. Jacob's reply on awakening from sleep is so familiar and so true to the human situation: "Surely the Lord is in this place; and I did not know it . . . . How awesome is this place! This is none other than the house of God, and this is the gate of heaven." The rock on which Jacob had pillowed his head during the night became the pillar of God's house in that place. Jacob did, in his own way, what Peter had suggested to Jesus on the mount of the Transfiguration, "Let us make here three booths, one for you and one for Moses and one for Elijah." Commitment to God is the one theme that emerges from this text and makes contact with the Gospel for the Day, in which Jesus declares to the disciples, "If any man would come after me, let him deny himself and take up his cross and follow me."

Romans 4:16-25 (C)

The first portion of this text (verses 13-18) was the second reading for Proper 5 (the Third Sunday after Pentecost) of Series/Cycle A, and most of the passage was the Roman Catholic and Lutheran reading for the same Sunday. See the *Lectionary Preaching Workbook, Cycle A*, for comments and suggestions.

Romans 5:1-11 (L)

The Roman Catholic, the Episcopal, and the Common lectionaries employ this selection as the second reading for the Third Sunday in Lent, Series/Cycle A. Comments may be found in the appropriate *Lectionary Preaching Workbook*.

Romans 8:31-34 (R); 8:31-39 (E)

The LBW lectionary used this text last Sunday, the First Sunday in Lent. "Liturgical adjustments" will have to be made by the pastor, as part of the pastoral exegetical process, to apply the commentary and sermon suggestions to the Second Sunday in Lent.

Mark 8:31-38 (E, L, C)

This Gospel is part of the incident in which Jesus, while on the way to the "village of Caesarea Philippi," asked two questions: First, "Who do men say that I am?" and second, "Who do you say that I am?" It was good old Peter who blurted out, "You are the Christ." Then, after charging them to tell no one, Jesus told them about his impending betrayal, suffering, death, and resurrection that would take place in Jerusalem. Peter wouldn't hear any of that and attempted to convince Jesus that this shouldn't happen. Thus the rebuke from Christ, "Get behind me, Satan! For you are not on the side of God, but of men." Jesus' mind was made up; he was convinced that this was God's will for him and nothing could change his mind — not even Satan himself. *Satan, in the person of Peter, was put down and totally defeated by Jesus once again.* At the end of the story, Jesus reveals the twist in the story. *Anyone who wants to be a disciple of Jesus has to be as totally commited to Christ and his mission as was Jesus himself. The followers of Jesus have to take up their crosses — what ever they may be — and serve the Lord.*

A Sermon on the Gospel, Mark 8:31-38 (E, L, C) — "Another Defeat for the Devil."

(Note: A sermon for this Sunday in *The Tree, the Tomb, and the Trumpet* concentrates on the first part of the text. This sermon is grounded in Jesus' question, "Who do you say that I am?" and his denunciation of Peter, "Get behind me, Satan! For you are not on the side of God, but of men.")

Peter's quick tongue had a way of getting him into trouble; it surely did on the occasion when Jesus said to him, "Who do you say that I am?" He blurted out, "You are the Christ." He would have been fine, had he stopped at that point and held his peace when Jesus told the disciples that he was going to die in Jerusalem. Mark doesn't say what he said in response to the information Jesus imparted to them, but he obviously attempted to dissuade Jesus from going to Jerusalem, at least from doing anything in public that would stir up the religious leaders and the temple priests. His argument, whatever it was, must have been persuasive. Why else would Jesus say to him, "Get behind me, Satan?" What an awful putdown to be called "Satan" by his teacher and master. That must have cut Peter to the quick.

1. *Jesus was tempted to turn his back upon Jerusalem when Peter tried to get him to change his mind.* The temptation must have been as real as when Jesus was enticed by Satan in the wilderness to abandon the will and plan of God and simply "to do his own thing." Satan never gives up!

2. *Jesus knew that there would be no service without sacrifice. Total commitment and complete obedience to God were requisite to the successful completion of his mission on earth — even if he had to sacrifice his life in the endeavor.*

3. *Jesus meant it when he said, "Get behind me, Satan," for the Evil One was, in his subtle manner, attempting to get to him.* (C. S. Lewis' *The Screwtape Letters* offers a number of illustrations on subtle temptation. That's what the whole book is about, in a sense.)

4. *Satan is always defeated when people simply say, "Get behind me, Satan."* He has to be conquered again and again, and he can be, because he knows that he will never conquer Jesus and those who believe in him.

5. *The final defeat of Satan came when Jesus died on the cross.* Only then was the victory over Satan, which began in the wilderness, complete.

A Sermon on the First Lesson, Genesis 17:1-10, 15-19 (C) — "A Covenant, a Child, and a Cross."

1. *The Covenant* — the Lord would be their God and they would be his people — forever.

2. *The Child* — promised by the Lord God and given a name by God himself. This is a pre-view of Christmas and the prophesy of Isaiah, "Unto us a child is born, to us a son is given; and the government will be upon his shoulder, and his name will be called 'Wonderful Counselor, Mighty God, Everlasting Father, Prince of Peace.' Of the increase of his government and of peace there will be no end . . . ."

3. *It took another child and a cross to renew the covenant and to establish and maintain peace once and for all.* There was no other way.

4. *Christ died to establish a new Covenant between God and his people.* That Covenant is made personal in our baptism, where we are sealed into that relationship by the Holy Spirit and "marked with the cross of Christ forever."

Genesis 22:1-2, 9-13, 15-18 (R); 22:1-14 (E)

See the comments and suggestions for last Sunday, the First Sunday in Lent, Cycle/Series A (LBW), which may be reworked for preaching on the Second Sunday in Lent.

Genesis 28:10-17 (18-22) (L) — "From Pillow to Pillar to Post."

1. *A stone pillow gave Jacob a dream instead of a headache.* He saw a ladder that stretched all the way to heaven, on which angels descended and ascended. God, he believed, was coming to him in a special way and trying to tell him something.

2. *The pillow became a pillar for Jacob recognized the reality of the dream and that special "presence" in that place.* "This is no other than the house of God, and this is the gate of heaven." So he promised to "let God be God," and be faithful to him as long as he lived.

3. *The pillar was replaced by a post.* Christ destroyed the religion of the temple, the old covenant that had beeen corrupted by people, and in its place put up a post — from whose crossbar he hung to renew the covenant and a right relationship between God and his creatures.

4. *From pillow to pillar to post* — that is the nature, according to this story, which reaches its climax in the New Testament, of our Lenten pilgrimage. And at the end of it, the post pries open the tomb, taking us — with Jesus — from death to life eternal.

A Sermon on the Second Lesson, Romans 4:16-25 (C)

The Third Sunday after Pentecost (Proper 5) *Lectionary Preaching Workbook, Cycle A*, has comments and a sermon suggestion for this text. See, also, the material for the Second Sunday in Lent, Cycle A, which overlaps the beginning of this text.

Romans 5:1-11 (L)

This text was explored and developed into a sermon suggestion for the Third Sunday in Lent (R, E, C), in the *Lectionary Preaching Workbook, Cycle A.*

Romans 8:31-34 (R); 8:31-39 (E)

The Lutheran lectionary has this text on the First Sunday in Lent, Cycle B. Comments and sermon suggestions apply to this Sunday, too.

Third Sunday in Lent

Roman Catholic	**Exodus 20:1-17**	**1 Corinthians 1:22-25**	**John 2:13-25**
Episcopal	**Exodus 20:1-17**	**Romans 7:13-25**	**John 2:13-22**
Lutheran	**Exodus 20:1-17**	**1 Corinthians 1:22-25**	**John 2:13-22**
Common	**Exodus 20:1-17**	**1 Corinthians 1:22-25**	**John 2:13-22**

The church year theological clue

In the ancient liturgy, this Sunday was known as *Oculi* — "Eyes" or "Vision" Sunday — from the fourteenth verse of Psalm 25, the Psalm that was also sung as the Introit on the Second Sunday in Lent: "My eyes are ever toward the Lord, for he shall pluck my feet out of the net." In the Gospel for the Day, John 2:13-22 (13-25 in the Roman missal), the cleansing of the temple supports the "vision" emphasis but with a twist: *The eyes of the people are opened by the Lord, who reveals himself as the replacement for the temple and its religion.* Perhaps it is this subtle shift from "My eyes are ever toward the Lord, for he shall pluck my feet out of the net" to a spiritual stance, wherein the people of God are observing what Jesus was doing when he cleansed the Temple that has caused several churches to abandon Psalm 25 (on both the Second and Third Sundays of Lent) and appoint different psalms for worship.

The Prayer of the Day

The LBW has prepared a collect that, more or less, "fits" the Gospel theme, as well as the Exodus 20 reading:

> *Eternal Lord, your kingdom has broken into our troubled world through the life, death, and resurrection of your Son. Help us to hear your word and obey it, so that we become instruments of your redeeming love; through your Son, Jesus Christ our Lord, who lives and reigns with you and the Holy Spirit, one God, now and forever.*

Obliquely, perhaps, but rather pointedly, this prayer pulls together the elements of response requisite to the hearing of the readings — and the sermon — for this Third Sunday in Lent. *Our ears have to be open to the word of the Lord, because we, in a sense, see through our ears.*

The Psalm of the Day

Psalm 19:7-10 (R); 19:7-14 (E, L) — This is one of the rare instances when three liturgical churches have appointed the same psalm as a responsory to the first reading. The reason is rather obvious: Psalm 19, at least the part selected for today's liturgy, is almost a perfect choice as a response to Exodus 20 and the giving of the Ten Commandments: "The Law of the Lord is perfect and revives the soul. The testimony of the Lord is sure and gives wisdom to the innocent. The statutes of the Lord are just and rejoice the heart; the commandment of the Lord is clear and gives light to the eyes. The fear of the Lord is clean and endures forever; the judgments of the Lord are true and righteous altogether. More to be desired are they than gold, more than much fine gold, sweeter far than honey, than honey in the comb." The last verse (14) articulates a proper response — not only of the preacher in the pulpit but also of the people in the pews — to the Law of God: "Let the words of my mouth and the meditations of my heart be acceptable in your sight, O Lord, my strength and my redeemer."

The Psalm Prayer (LBW)

> *Heavenly Father, you have filled the world with beauty. Open our eyes to see your gracious hand in all your works, that rejoicing in your whole creation, we may*

learn to serve you with gladness, for the sake of him through whom all things were made, your Son, Jesus Christ our Lord.

(Note: Unfortunately, this prayer focuses on the theme of the first part of the psalm, God's gracious work of creation.)

The readings:

Several churches were unanimous in their choice of a first reading for this Sunday, even down to the exact verses of the text. It is the account of the giving of the Ten Commandments to Moses, which the various churches "count" in different ways. The Roman Catholic and Lutheran methods combine two through four into the first commandment. Anglicans and others denote verse 4 as the second commandment. They also compress the ninth and tenth commandments into a single unity, unlike the Roman Catholic and Lutheran churches, which separate verse 17 into two "covet" commandments. But it is the part that the commandments play in the life of the Christian that matters, not the "counting." They have always been important — and valid, in one way or another — for Christians. They are not only to be used in catechetical instructions, but also in worship and preaching, and they need to be preached in the churches. William Carl III, in an excellent article, "The Decalogue in Liturgy, Preaching, and Life" (in *Interpretation*, Vol. 43, No. 3, July 1989) writes:"To live the complete Christian life through the cycle of conviction of sin, repentance, justification, sanctification, obedience, and hope is to experience the Decalogue in its fullness through Christ in the worship, preaching, and spiritual and moral witness in the community of believers in the world."

(Note: Those preachers who intend to preach on this first reading would do well to read the four essays on the Decalogue in Volume 43. The other three are by Patrick D. Miller, Jr., Reginald Fuller, and David C. Steinmetz.)

1 Corinthians 1:22-25 (R, L, C)

In this, his first letter to the church at Corinth, Paul wastes no time getting to the heart of the Gospel. He is aware of the difference in spiritual perception of the Jews and the Gentiles/Greeks: the Jews "demand signs" and the Greeks "seek wisdom." Jews want to know that God is in charge and what it is that he is doing in the world, while the Greeks of Paul's time wanted to make sense of the world and the part human beings have in any divine plan. Paul believes that God "has made foolish the wisdom of the world," and he tells this to the Corinthian congregation. He has done this through the death and resurrection of Jesus Christ, a mystery which no one can fully penetrate and which remains, therefore, a *scandal* to the Jews and *foolishness* to the Greeks. The people of the world today are not much different and they line up on either side of the cross. But those who stand before the cross in faith know that Jesus Christ is the *power of God* and the *wisdom of God*, who works through the Gospel for the salvation of all people.

Romans 7:13-25 (E)

This is the exercise of self-examination of one who stands before the law of the Lord and, specifically, the commandments. He knows that he loves the law, but he cannot keep it. He desires to keep it perfectly, but he cannot — something inside him ("nothing good dwells within me, that is, my flesh"). Paul confesses: "For I do not do the good I want, but the evil I do not want is what I do." The law, in other words, convicts him of sin and of dwelling in "this body of death." He can do nothing else but cry out to God for deliverance and he finds his answer in Jesus Christ and his cross. Therefore he is able to say, "Thanks be to God through Jesus Christ our Lord!" — to which believers, who had the same experience with the law and sin that Paul had, may add "Amen."

John 2:13-22 (E, L, C); 2:13-25 (R)

As always, John tells the same story of and about Jesus. In this pericope, he describes the cleansing of the temple, but he does it in his own way. For one thing, he puts this incident, with its encounter with the religious authorities, at the very beginning of Jesus' ministry instead of during his last week of life in Jerusalem. He also predicted, along with Mark, that the temple would soon be destroyed. John added some details to the story: The whip Jesus used to drive out the people who were desecrating the temple, the quotation from Psalm 69 ("Zeal for your house has eaten me up"), and the statement about the length of time (forty-six years) it took to build the temple.

John arranged the story as he did, and added the details he considered to be significant, to show what the shape of Jesus' ministry really was to be. Right at the start of the story, he laid the groundwork for the violent reaction and religious indignation on the part of the Jewish leaders which would lead to his death. Jesus came into the world as "the Word became flesh and dwelt among us" to engage in a God-given mission to deliver humanity from sin and death, and that mission would cost him his life. But, even more important, at the start of his ministry, is the news that he has come to destroy the religion of the temple. His crucified and resurrected body would replace it — "Destroy this temple, and in three days I will raise it up." And that is what happened, although it was a few decades later (about four that the temple was totally destroyed by the Romans, his glorified body was raised up in three days, as he said it would be. If "destroy this body" were a challenge to the Jews, John makes it rather evident that they will soon take him up on it and, somehow or other, see to his destruction.

A Sermon on the Gospel, John 2:13-22 (E, L, C); 2:13-25 (R) — "Ultimate Madness."

It is one thing to contend that one is ready to die, but it is quite a different matter to dare people with power over life and death to take one's life away. "Sometimes I wish the good Lord would take me out of this life; I have so many problems to deal with that life is impossible." A middle-aged woman, divorced and on a disability pension, which terminates when she becomes sixty-five years of age, said that recently. She really meant it. Her Social Security payments will be far less than the money she now receives for her disability (a combination of Social Security and a private fund). She sees her life becoming unmanageable when she attains sixty-five years of age. Her financial picture could be even more dismal, if the condition that put her on disability, in the first place, worsens. "Sometimes I wish the Lord would take me . . . ." But that's not all that there is to her life; there are other times when life still seems good and worthwhile.

But Jesus, healthy and in the prime of his life, dared the religious authorities to take his life, utterly to destroy his body, adding the ridiculous claim, "Destroy this temple, *and in three days I will raise it.*" Only a madman would say something like that. And so, before the end of the story, they took him at his word and tried to do just that.

1. *Tear down the temple* with its out-moded religious system and its corrupt leadership. That was what Jesus was about to embark upon in his brief ministry. His teaching, and preaching, miracles and and ministry completely undermined the foundations of the Jewish religion with its sacrificial system. The "temple" just had to fall. Jesus, not the Romans, really destroyed it.

2. *Jesus came preaching and teaching about a new way* to worship the Lord God. He offered a new covenant — one written in blood and pain as he hung upon Calvary's cross. A single sacrifice would suffice, he preached during his ministry, and gain forgiveness and reconciliation for all who accepted it and believe him to be the Son of God, the savior of the world.

3. *In what must have seemed like sheer madness to any who understood him, he challenged,* "Destroy this temple, and in three days I will raise it." The religious leaders were smart enough to figure out what he was talking about; only a fool would say something like that —

and he certainly wasn't talking like a mad magician, who might think he could work the ultimate magic trick by restoring a building that had taken forty-six years to build. Some of them must have figured out that he was talking about his own body, his own death.

4. *His challenge finally led to his crucifixion* — and, through the power of God, he made good on his prediction. The temple, his body, was raised up, and we remember and celebrate the fact that, through baptism, we have been made members of that body in life and in death — forever.

A Sermon on the First Lesson, Exodus 20:1-17 — "The Dilemma of the Decalogue."

(Note: It is impossible to preach a sermon in which all of the Ten Commandments are presented in detail; it would simply be too long. One approach would be to preach on the first commandment — over against Jesus' "new commandment I give you . . . ." Another possibility would be to develop a sermon series on the Ten Commandments for Lent, but the logistics of such a series might be a bit complicated. A third way to deal homiletically with this text would be to discuss how the Ten Commandments intertwine with the Christian life. How one does this will be determined by one's denominational affiliation and one's personal theological interpretation of the relationship of law and Gospel. This will be the approach taken in his suggestion.)

William Carl tells how Dennis Kinlaw, who once was an Old Testament professor at Asbury Theological Seminary and president of Asbury College, questioned a boy named Tommy, who was something of a spitting image of the rich young ruler in the Gospel. He thought he had kept all of the commandments — perfectly. "I (Kinlaw) said: 'Wait a minute, Tommy. Tell me anybody you've ever met that without the power of Christ in his or her life who has ever kept the Ten Commandments.' You know what that rascal did? He looked me straight in the eye and said, 'I'm not so bad.' So I rose to the challenge and said, 'Tommy, which one did you ever keep?' And he said, 'Which one did I ever break?' I said, 'Do you enjoy praying?' He said, 'Not particularly.' I said, 'Well, there goes the first one. Because, you see, when it says you're not supposed to have any gods before him that means in your affection and your communion.' "

Carl says that Kinlaw went through each commandment, saying to the boy. "There goes another one." When he got to number seven, this is what happened: 'I looked at him and said, 'Tommy, did you ever tell a dirty story with relish or listen to one with pleasure?' And the rascal looked back at me and said, 'Did you?' And I said, 'There goes another one.' I said, 'Tommy, did you ever take anything that didn't belong to you? Either a possession or maybe a test, cheating a bit?' He said, 'Of course.' I said, 'There goes another one.' I said, 'Did you ever get in a tight spot and when you told the story you shaded it just a little bit to make you look better?' He said, 'Why, of course.' I said, 'There goes another one.'

"Kinlaw got him on the last one, too, and then said, 'Tommy, which one of these did you ever keep?' The boy looked back at the Old Testament professor, his eyes flushed full, and he said, 'Sir, am I in that bad a shape?' " (Dennis Kinlaw told this in a sermon, which William Carl heard or read, at Salem Camp Meeting, Covington, Georgia, in August 1988.) One possibility is to expand this a bit into a narrative sermon, as suggested by Richard Jenson, in his *Teaching the New Testament.*

1. *The dilemma of the Decalogue* is simply that we can't, try as we may, keep the Ten Commandments — and save ourselves.

2. *The Ten Commandments, therefore, convict us of our sin* and make us realize that we need to seek God's mercy and forgiveness, which he gives us in Christ.

3. *But Jesus demands that we be perfect,* even giving us a new commandment to obey — "Love one another as I have loved you." Living the new life in Christ, through Baptism, grace, and the power of the Holy Spirit, we are to be obedient to the commands of God and the teachings of Jesus Christ.

4. *That drives us to our knees with a "mea culpa" every single day of our lives* — and the wonder of it is that God lifts us up each time to that new life in Christ that is ours from time to eternity.

A Sermon on the Second Lesson, 1 Corinthians 1:22-25 (R, L, C) — "Wise Guy."

1. This is a person who thinks that the Christian religion has only to do with the quality of life here on earth.

2. This is a person who thinks that, if God is real, the Lord will give special signs to convince him/her of his reality, presence, and power.

3. This is the person who says, "There is no God." All of this happened by chance.

4. This is the person who looks at the cross and declares, "Jesus was a fool. He allowed himself to be martyred out of some misguided notion of divinity."

5. The wise person is one who hears the Gospel, considers the cross and resurrection, and says, "My Lord and my God."

Romans 7:13-25 (E) — "Helpless, but not Hopeless."

1. That's how Paul really sees himself. He does not do the good he would, because his sinful self takes over and causes him to break the commandments of God.

2. There's a war going on within Paul — and within every one of us. Our will and intentions are engaged in a death struggle with our sinful nature, which is poised to win the war.

3. Thanks to God the war has been won — Jesus has come to our aid in the battle and he has won it! But he had to die to do it. And for that — and our deliverance and forgiveness — we offer him our heartfelt thanks and devotion.

Fourth Sunday of Lent

Roman Catholic	2 Chronicles 36:14-17, 19-23	Ephesians 2:4-10	John 3:14-21
Episcopal	2 Chronicles 36:14-23	Ephesians 2:4-10	John 3:14-21
Lutheran	Numbers 21:4-9	Ephesians 2:4-10	John 3:14-21
Common	2 Chronicles 36:14-23	Ephesians 2:4-10	John 3:14-21

The church year theological clue

Under the classic plan of the church year, the Fourth Sunday in Lent brought the second section of Lent (the first section of Lent was, in effect, the three "gesima" Sundays) to a close and prepared the way for *Judica* (Passion Sunday) and the beginning of passion-tide two weeks before Easter. This Sunday was known as *Laetare* — a kind of rejoicing Sunday, as the psalm/introit indicates: "Rejoice ye with Jerusalem,and be glad with her: all ye that love her. Rejoice for joy with her; all ye that mourn for her. I was glad when they said unto me: Let us go into the house of the Lord." The psalm employed in the Introit is Psalm 122, a pilgrimage that catches the spirit of the ascent of the people of Israel who are going up to Jerusalem for Passover. Used in this Christian context, in the middle of Lent, it reminds the New Israel that Easter lies ahead and provides time for spiritual refreshment for the remainder of the Lenten journey. It was known by parts of the church as "Refreshment Sunday."

The Fourth Sunday in Lent continues to be mid-Lent and, like the "gesima" Sundays, ought to be a reminder — and therefore a source of joy and refreshment — for the people of God of the proximity of Easter and its "gladness." The readings, especially the second reading and the Gospel for this year, remind the faithful that they have a reason for rejoicing — they have already been delivered from sin and death by Jesus Christ. Charged up with joy in the Gospel, they are able to move ahead and and face up to the passion and death of the Lord. Lent is half completed, and Easter is almost at hand, so God's people rejoice *as they should on every Sunday and every day of their lives.*

The Prayer of the Day

The classic collect "fits" the traditional theme of this Sunday — rejoicing in the salvation provided by the Lord God to all who call Christ their Lord and Savior — better than the contemporary prayers. "Grant, we beseech thee, Almighty God, that we, who for our evil deeds deserve to be punished, by the comfort of thy grace may mercifully be relieved." In the LBW contemporary prayers, one word — the last — misses the theme of this Sunday and the point of the readings: "God of all mercy, by your power to heal and to forgive, graciously cleanse us from all sin and make us strong." "Make us *rejoice* in our salvation" would help the prayer function more properly on this Sunday.

The Psalm of the Day

Psalm 27:1-9 (10-18) (L) — In the LBW, this psalm is also appointed for the Third Sunday after the Epiphany, where it serves the manifestation theme of Epiphany quite well: "The Lord is my light and my salvation; whom then shall I fear?" As it is used this second time in the liturgical cycle, it points to the latter part of the Gospel for the Day, where John declares that "the light has come into the world" in Jesus Christ. The sinful estate of mankind is described — and quite properly for Lent — with "and men loved darkness rather than light, because their deeds were evil." Verses 10-18, which are optional, articulate the plea of a penitent sinner:

> *Hearken to my voice, O Lord, when I call; have mercy on me and answer me. You speak in my heart and say, 'Seek my face.' Your face, Lord, will I seek. Hide not your face from me, nor turn away your servant in displeasure . . . . Oh, tarry and await the Lord's pleasure; be strong, and he shall comfort your heart; wait patiently for the Lord.*

Psalm 122 (E) — The pilgrims probably rehearsed this psalm as they made their way to Jerusalem to celebrate Passover, and they sang this song with excitement and joy as they entered the Holy City and the environs of the Temple. It was selected by the Episcopal Church for at least two reasons: 1.) it sounds the note of rejoicing that traditionally marks the Fourth Sunday in Lent, thus it is something of a liturgical remnant; 2.) it contains the biblical notion that Jerusalem is the city where all of the nations of the world will, in time, go up to their salvation and peace. Therefore, an eschatological emphasis has always been read into this psalm in its liturgical usage.

Psalm 137:1-6 — A fitting response to the first reading is offered in this psalm, which speaks about the exile and the reasons for it. Without the psalm, the first reading would be totally out of thematic harmony with the other readings for this Sunday. As it is, two sections of the biblical propers fit together — the first reading and the psalm. The Roman Catholic Church employs it for another reason: it pictures the situation of the people of God attempting to keep Lent. Repentant sinners can say with the Israelites in their captivity: "By the waters of Babylon we sat down and wept, when we remembered you, O Zion. . . . If I forget you, O Jerusalem, let my right hand forget its skill. Let my tongue cleave to the roof of my mouth if I do not remember you, if I do not set Jerusalem above my highest joy."

The Psalm Prayer — Psalm 137 (LBW)

Heavenly Father, you willed to make us citizens of your country and singers of your mercy. Do not abandon us in the land of exile, but bring us to the heavenly Jerusalem chanting your praise; through Jesus Christ our Lord.

The readings:

2 Chronicles 36:14-17, 19-23 (R); 36:14-23 (E, C)

One of the strangest selections in the lectionary, this reading has nothing to connect it to the Sunday nor to the second and third readings. Reginald Fuller suggests — tongue-in-cheek, I am sure — that Psalm 137 was chosen first, and only then was the first reading selected. (Oddly enough, the *Book of Common Prayer*, on whose lectionary committee he had served, has retained the first reading on this Fourth Sunday in Lent, but changed the psalm.) The agony of Israel — punished by the invading army, which slew young and old alike, desecrated and burned the temple, and carried off those remaining into exile in Babylon — is articulated in this reading. The only positive note comes at the conclusion of the reading (and the book) when the chronicler relates how Cyrus, King of Persia, was moved by God to allow the Jews to return to Jerusalem. Verses 22 and 23 are the exact duplicates of the opening verses of Ezra 1:1-3. The typology of the reading, suggesting crucifixion and resurrection, has to be the reason that this reading was selected for this Sunday.

Numbers 21:4-9 (L)

This reading, quite unlike the previous one, was chosen because it connects with the Gospel for the Day. It speaks about the impatience and discontent of the people of Israel with Moses and with God himself as they journeyed through the wilderness on their way to the Promised Land. The Lord sent a plague of fiery serpents among the people, and those who escaped death repented of their sins. They asked Moses to petition the Lord to take away the serpents, and Moses did just that. He prayed to God for the people. At God's direction, Moses made a fiery serpent and put it on a pole, and when anyone who had been bitten by a snake looked at it, that person was immediately healed. The Gospel for the Day recites part of that story just before the famous "God so loved the world" theme is spelled out by John. The Christian, who remembers how Christ was lifted up, should rejoice "without ceasing" — especially in the middle of Lent.

Ephesians 2:4-10

Whoever wrote this epistle was obviously a disciple of Paul. In this lection, his theology is genuinely Pauline when he says twice (once parenthetically) "For by grace you have been saved." He adds, ". . . through faith; and this is not your own doing, it is the gift of God — not because of works, lest any man should boast." Many scholars believe that this is a portion of a baptismal hymn, possibly the same hymn that provides a theological background for similar theological assertions in Romans and Colossians. And despite the fact that the author declares that (in baptism) he has "raised us up with him, and made us sit with him in the heavenly places in Christ Jesus," he saves himself from gnosticism by insisting that the "raised" Christian has been "created in Christ Jesus for good works." The works do not save people, but should issue forth spontaneously as a consequence of salvation and an expression of faith in the Lord Jesus Christ. (See Herman Stuempfle's *Preaching Law and Gospel* for more on works as a consequence of redemption.)

John 3:14-21

The "Gospel in a nutshell," is John 3:16 — "For God so loved the world that he gave his only Son, that whoever believes in him should not perish but have eternal life." But it does not stand by itself, it follows the incident in which Nicodemus visited Jesus and heard Jesus' speech: "Truly, truly, I say to you, unless one is born anew, he cannot see the kingdom of God." The last verse of that speech is the first verse of the Gospel for the Day: "And as Moses lifted up the serpent in the wilderness, so must the Son of man be lifted up, that whoever believes in him may have eternal life." After Jesus responds to three questions from Nicodemus, John launches into his "For God so loved the world" theology, which moves into the light/darkness motif — deliverance and judgment — that John had introduced in the first chapter of his Gospel. The uniqueness of this lection is the connection between Moses and the serpent, and Jesus and the cross. There is power in the loving deed accomplished by Christ's dying and being lifted up to create faith in those who hear of God's love and who look upon the Christ on the cross for forgiveness and deliverance. It is at this point that the "God so loved the world" theme is perceived concretely by the faithful. And it is obvious that the combination of second reading and Gospel press the preacher to proclaim this positive action of a loving God in Christ's suffering and death on the cross.

A Sermon on the Gospel, John 3:14-21 — "Salvation Hangs on a Tree."

As I was writing this piece, my visiting granddaughter, Rachel, came into my study and looked over my shoulder at what I was typing. She saw the "Gospel in a nut shell" line and said, "Grandpa, do you know what we did last Christmas? We took walnuts, hollowed them out, wrote 'John 3:16' — the Gospel in a Nut Shell' on a small piece of paper, crumpled it up, put it in the empty shell, and then glued the top and bottom together. Then we hung it on our Christmas tree as an ornament to represent the Gospel." I suppose this has been done by many people on many other occasions, but the important thing is that the symbolism is correct and concrete. The Gospel — our salvation — hangs on a tree in the person of the suffering and dying Son of God, even Jesus Christ the Lord.

1. *The cross is a concrete symbol of God's gracious love for his people.* There is no more startling or graphic symbol than a cross with the suffering and dying Savior upon it.

People who visit the two chapels on the campus of Luther Northwestern Theological Seminary often remark about the impact of the smaller chapel, the Chapel of the Cross. (The larger chapel is the Chapel of the Incarnation.) The main reason, it seems to me, is that almost right in the middle of it is Paul Granlund's sculpture of the *Christ Figure*. It depicts a Jesus who has suffered horribly and is drawn up in a near fetal position in death. Jesus is dead! He is high and lifted up in the middle of the faithful who worship in that place, and were it not for the fact that they know that the crucified Christ is also the risen

Lord, present in Word and Sacrament, the sculpture would be too overpowering for the worshipers. In the newer and larger Chapel of the Incarnation, a beautifully created "stick cross" (a crucifix made entirely out of small pieces of wood and metal) hangs just inside the main entrance and overlooks the baptismal font standing in front of it. Each, in its own way, makes a statement about the love of God in Jesus Christ.

2. *God gives his Son — and salvation — to the world on that cross.* The Tree of Death for Jesus is the Tree of Life for repentant sinners. God's salvation hangs on a tree for all to see.

3. *The Tree reaches all the way to Heaven itself.* It connects time and eternity, the faithful and God — and it separates the light from the darkness.

Salvador Dali's "Christ of St. John of the Cross" is another concrete symbol of salvation in the cross of Jesus Christ. This is how I used it in a sermon in *The Tree, the Tomb, and the Trumpet* (p. 33): "I remember Douglas Webster's book, *In Debt to Christ (A Study in the Meaning of the Cross).* As the reader opens it to the title page — and before another word is read — Salvador Dali's 'Christ of St. John of the Cross' meets the eye. The cross is huge and lifted up so that it seems to be floating over the earth. Christ hangs there, looking down — a strong young man, in the prime of his life, nailed to the terrible Tree. Light emanates from the base of the cross, illuminating the darkness of the night and casting the first rays of a new day's rays upon the earth. Blue sky is seen above a lake, and a fishing boat has been beached directly under the cross of Christ; two fishermen are working on their nets, while a dim figure can be seen walking toward them along the waterfront. Webster says, 'He (Jesus) is the "young Prince of Glory" as in the original version of Isaac Watts' famous hymn. He seems to be holding back the great volume of darkness, forcing its retreat . . . . But the Cross remains, dominating the world, and the world the artist sees is the world on which Christ looks from His Cross.' "

4. *The gift is received by faith, which in itself is another gift of God.* The faithful know that they are forgiven and thank God for the gift. Look at that Tree — at the salvation hanging there in the crucified Christ — and live.

A Sermon on the First Lesson, 2 Chronicles 36:14-17, 19-23 (R); 36:14-23 (E, C) — "The Return of the Remnant."

1. *The remnant in exile* — both priest and people sinned and God caused them to fall before the army of the Chaldeans and to be carted off to Babylon.

2. *God relents* — causing Cyrus the King of the Persians to agree to set free the remnant of God's people and allow them to return to Jerusalem.

3. *The repentant return* — to Jerusalem and to their God to rebuild his house in the Holy City.

4. *The remnant and Lent* — a time to repent of sin, to return to the Lord, to renew the baptismal covenant, and to praise the risen Lord in word and deed.

Numbers 21:4-9 (L) — "A New Use for a Pole."

1. *God ordered Moses to make a fiery serpent and to put it on a pole where the snake-bitten Israelites might see it — and live.* Oddly enough, he didn't tell him to make a club and smash every snake in sight. He put the symbol of a snake on a pole — and that was the new way to overcome snake bites.

2. *God allowed Christ to be nailed to a pole and to die hanging there for all the world to see.* Salvation was nailed to a pole. That was a new use for a pole. God might have made the pole into a "club" and used it to eradicate the sinful from the world, but he didn't.

3. *God displayed his love for humanity and his offer of eternal life to the believers — on a pole.* That's a strange way of offering himself to his people and a new use for a pole.

4. *Like the Israelites, all people have to do is look at that pole in repentance and faith to live.*

1. That's what God did. He saved us by grace, not by our works and good deeds, but in Jesus Christ.

2. That's the only way that God could save us — by his amazing love that knows no. limits whatsoever. He wants to save every single human being on earth.

3. That's why he expects us to respond in love, to serve him, obey him, and to do good works in the name of Jesus Christ — because he has saved us at the cross.

4. That's why we do the only thing we can — love him, thank him, and live for him in the world.

Fifth Sunday in Lent

Roman Catholic   Jeremiah 31:31-34   Hebrews 5:7-9   John 12:20-23
Episcopal   Jeremiah 31:31-34   Hebrews 5:(1-4), 5-10   John 12:20-33
Lutheran   Jeremiah 31:31-34   Hebrews 5:7-9   John 12:20-33
Common   Jeremiah 31:31-34   Hebrews 5:7-9   John 12:20-33

The church year theological clue

More than any other Sunday in Lent, the fifth Sunday has lost its theological and liturgical identity. Prior to the liturgical revisions which followed Vatican II, the Fifth Sunday in Lent was known as *Judica* (from the first verse of the Introit, Psalm 43) and marked the beginning of the two weeks Passiontide, that concentrated on the passion, suffering, and death of the Lord Jesus. Theologically, the emphasis was on the mystery of the cross, which was proclaimed in the readings and celebrated in the liturgical activities of the third period of Lent. Concentration upon the reality and meaning of the death of Jesus was intensified, so that this week became a preparation for Holy Week and the sacred Triduum of Holy Thursday, Good Friday, and Holy Saturday.

All of that has been changed now. The Sunday of the Passion now occurs on the Sixth Sunday in Lent, reducing the period for observing the Passion of the Lord to one week. The Fifth Sunday in Lent, therefore, is simply another Sunday in Lent. It retains the theological character of every Sunday — that is, it is a celebration of the death and resurrection of the Lord. It gets its themes from Lent itself, but also from the lessons appointed for the day. In Cycle/Series B, the attention of the church is brought to bear upon the *obedience of Christ to the will of the Father* (which cost him his life), and also upon *the power of the cross to draw people to the Savior* in whom they will experience the forgiveness of their sins.

The Prayer of the Day

The classic collect has been replaced (rather than reworded) by the various churches so that it will be more in line with the worship of the people on this day. The Episcopal Church has rewritten an older collect that fits the ''new'' Sunday and the times we live in:

> *Almighty God, you alone can bring into order the unruly wills and affections of sinners: Grant your people grace to love what you command and desire what you promise; that among the swift and varied changes of the world, our hearts may surely there be fixed where true joys are to be found; through Jesus Christ our Lord, who lives and reigns with you and the Holy Spirit, one God, now and for ever. Amen*

The Psalm of the Day

Psalm 51:1-2, 10-13 (R); 51, or 51:11-16 (E); 51:11-16 (L) — The use of this Psalm in Series/Cycle B places worshipers in the context of Ash Wednesday once again. Many of the Ash Wednesday liturgies include the singing — or recitation — of Psalm 51 in a service of public confession. It is truly a penitential psalm, purportedly the work of David when he fully realizes the gravity of the sins he has committed against Bathsheba and Uriah. But it accommodates the spiritual condition of every human being who becomes aware of his/her unworthiness before God (which is the reason why it is part of nearly every service of confession):

> *Have mercy upon me, O God, according to your loving kindness; in your great compassion, blot out my sin . . . . Wash me [a baptismal motif] through and through from my wickedness, and cleanse me from my sin . . . . For I know my transgressions, and my sin is ever before me.*

The last half of the psalm — without the verses that lead up to the rebuilding of the walls of Jerusalem (18-20) which are omitted in most of the lectionaries and missals — concentrates on a plea for forgiveness: "Hide your face from my sins, and blot out all my iniquities." But it goes beyond a plea for total pardon, asking — in the spirit of Lent and Easter — that God engage in an act of recreation, so that a totally new creature might emerge from this penitential experience: "Create in me a clean heart, O God, and renew a right spirit within me. Cast me not away from your presence, and take not your Holy Spirit from me."

These two verses were the offertory most often sung in the Common Service of the Lutheran Church. They begin the last half of the service, the Eucharist, or Holy Communion. Many Lutheran congregations continue to sing this offertory. It is unfortunate that the following verses, especially verse 14, have been omitted — "I shall teach your ways to the wicked, and sinners shall return to you . . . . Open my lips, O Lord, and my mouth shall proclaim your praise." The latter verse (16) is retained as the opening word of Morning Prayer by Lutherans, but Morning Prayer is not widely used in parishes. This psalm makes it clear that penitent pilgrims, attempting to keep Lent and who have their eyes fixed on the cross, must recognize the sinlessness of Christ over their own sinfulness, and plead with God for forgiveness and new life.

The Psalm Prayer (LBW)

Almighty and merciful Father, you freely forgave those who, as David of old, acknowledge and confess their sins. Create in us pure hearts, and wash away all our sins in the blood of your dear Son, Jesus Christ our Lord.

The readings:

Jeremiah 31:31-34

This reading was originally appointed for the First Sunday of Advent in various older lectionaries. It is more appropriate on the Fifth Sunday of Lent, when the cross event is about to be scrutinized and celebrated by the faithful, because it talks about a new covenant that God will make with his people. Jeremiah was telling this to the exiles in Babylon, a covenant that will be engraved on the hearts of his people, rather than upon stone tablets as in the past. The reading, which declares, "I will be their God, and they shall be my people," predicts that all people will "know the Lord," and God's promise to "forgive their iniquity, and I will remember their sin no more." The church has — almost from the beginning of the Christian era — interpreted this reading as finding its fulfillment in the passion and death of Jesus Christ. God did make that new covenant with his people — at and on the cross of Christ. The cross accomplishes what God intended, and it will last forever.

Hebrew 5:7-9 (R, L, C); 5:(1-4), 5-10 (E)

This little snippet of an epistle is part of the author's argument that Jesus is a high priest after the order of Melchizedek. He did not seek the priestly function on his own, but God himself had said of Jesus, "This is my beloved Son; listen to him." The prayers and cries, to which the writer of Hebrews refers, are undoubtedly those which Jesus uttered in Gethsemane when he asked God to — if possible — remove the cup he had to drink. He knew that God's will had to be done, and although God heard his prayer in the garden, he did not deliver him from death on a cross. He did, however, raise him up and complete the redemption that Jesus had come to do through his resurrection. It is in this — Jesus' perfect obedience, even unto death — that the author sees the perfection of Jesus Christ completed by the Father.

John 12:20-33

It almost seems as though Jesus summarily dismissed the request of the Greeks, who had said to Philip, "We would see Jesus." Jesus responds when the request is relayed to him with an announcement about his impending death. First, the time appointed by God is at hand; he will die very soon. Second, he informs the disciples that it is necessary for him to die in order to accomplish God's purpose of delivering all people — Jews and Gentiles — from their sins. And third, he makes it perfectly clear that he can only be "seen" — that is perceived as the Savior — only after he is crucified and resurrected from the dead. In the middle of Jesus' explanation, when he says, "Father, glorify thy name," God speaks and declares, "I have glorified it, and I will glorify it again." Jesus believed that the disciples needed to hear this, and that they had to know not only that he would die, but also that he would die by crucifixion. So in the statement Jesus made to the disciples, it is clear that it can only be after the crucifixion and the resurrection that Jesus will be "seen" by the Greeks and other Gentiles. Then they will understand the whole story, and the story will give them new life in the Lord.

A Sermon on the Gospel, John 12:20-33 — "Born to Die and Live."

Some people seem to be born to suffer and die, and their fate makes no sense to us. One of my younger brothers was such a person. At age twelve he began to have pains in his legs and was treated for various things for three years before his condition was diagnosed as rheumatic fever. Soon he developed a severe case of arthritis, had to drop out of high school, and saw his ambition to become a golf professional vanish in pain and frustration. From the time he was nine or ten years of age, he had spent all of his spare time at a local golf course. He looked for lost golf balls on his way to school, and by twelve years of age he was learning how to be a caddy, as well as how to play golf. But when his arthritis became severe, he received experimental treatment (which did him no good) and in time moved to Arizona in the hope that the dry climate would be beneficial to his health. It wasn't, and he died — tragically — at thirty-six years of age.

Our Lord was probably a bit younger than that when he told his disciples that he had to die, and that the hour of his death was at hand. He said to them, "For this purpose *[to die a terrible death]* I have come into the world." I'm certain that he prayed more than once, "Father, save me from this hour" — but it wasn't to be. His comfort came in the knowledge that the Father was with him, and in the assurance that God would see him through the awful experience. "Father," he had prayed to God, "glorify thy name." And God spoke out, "I have glorified it and I will glorify it again." With confidence in this knowledge, he could say, "and I, when I am lifted up from the earth, will draw all men to myself."

1. *All people come to earth to live and die; Jesus came to earth to die and live.* God had revealed to him that his death was necessary if human beings and God were to be reconciled to one another. *God planned that Jesus would die to save the human race from annihilation.*

2. *His death on the cross would be recognized — after the resurrection — as the action God took not only to save people, but to enable them to comprehend the love that he has for his creatures.* God will do anything he has to — even sacrifice his Son — in order to save his people from sin and death.

3. *The death of Jesus has power to draw people to the crucified risen Lord as their Savior whenever, and wherever, the sacred story — the Good News — is told.* It is in the word, the gospel story, that God's mighty action continues, causing people to contemplate the cross and believe that Jesus is their Lord and Savior.

4. So many people have died at a young age (my brother among them) when they wanted to live long and useful lives. *Jesus was born to die when he did* — also at a young age — so that he would live forever as the risen ascended Lord, whose cross would bring believers to him that he might take them into the everlasting Kingdom of God.

A Sermon on the First Lesson, Jeremiah 31:31-34 — "Christ and the New Covenant."

1. The old covenant was too much for human beings to keep. The law of God, broken by everyone, brought condemnation upon Jews and, later, upon the Gentile world.

2. God had to find a way to renew the covenant, or else he had to destroy the human race. He loved his people too much to do that, despite their infidelity and waywardness.

3. The only way that God could be faithful to himself and to human beings was to take drastic action to renew the covenant — and he did that through the cross of Christ. That day the New Covenant began with the advent of Jesus into the world.

4. God has written that covenant in our hearts through his word and the sacraments. Our business is to thank, praise, serve, and obey him.

A Sermon on the Second Lesson, Hebrews 5:7-9 (R, L, C) — "An Apparently Futile Prayer."

1. By the time we reach middle-age, most of us have had an experience in which prayer seems to have been futile. It might have seemed that God didn't hear our prayer, or that he had refused to grant our petition, or even that he had no power to do anything about the situation. We wonder if there is any point in praying at all.

2. Jesus' prayer, "Father, save me from this hour," seems to be one of those futile prayers. He was destined to die, despite the prayer to the One who said, "You are my beloved Son." What kind of a Heavenly Father would allow his Son to die such a seemingly unnecessary death?

3. The prayer of that soon-to-die man was heard because God answered him when he asked the Lord God to glorify his name: "I have glorified it [his name], and I will glorify it again."

4. And God did glorify his name in Jesus — on the cross, on the third day when the tomb was empty, and on that day when he received him into heaven and placed him at his right hand to share in the eternal glory.

4. That is the Christ who seemed to pray a futile prayer, but whose prayer was really answered by Almighty God. He answers our seemingly futile prayers, too, and delivers us from our worst enemies, death and the Devil.

Sunday of the Passion

Roman Catholic	Isaiah 50:4-7	Philippians 2:6-11	Mark 14:1—15:47
Episcopal	Isaiah 45:21-25	Philippians 2:5-11	Mark 11:1-11a, 14:32-72,
	or Isaiah 52:13—53:12		15:1-39 (40-47)
Lutheran	Zechariah 9:9-10	Philippians 2:5-11	Mark 11:1-10, 14:1—15:47
			or Mark 15:1-39
Common	Isaiah 50:4-9a	Philippians 2:5-11	Mark 11:1-11

The church year theological clue

The transfer of the Sunday of the Passion from the Fifth Sunday in Lent to the Sixth Sunday in Lent (Palm Sunday) represents a return to one of the earliest practices in the church. Palm Sunday was celebrated as part of the observation of the first day of Holy Week, or the Passion of Our Lord. First in Jerusalem, then in other parts of the church, the entire Passion story was read on this Sunday. The other three gospel narratives of the Passion were read during Holy Week, so that the "history of the Passion" was proclaimed at least four times during this pivotal week. The Gospel of St. Matthew announced the Passion on Sunday and the echo of that story was heard three more times during the week. Most lectionaries today have only one echo — on Good Friday — when the Passion may be read from St. John. This is not all bad since *the liturgical/theological function of the Sunday of the Passion was to point to Good Friday and the events of the crucifixion.*

Theologically, the Sunday of the Passion thrusts the great mystery of Jesus' betrayal, trial, condemnation, suffering, and death on the cross for the redemption of human beings by God before the faithful so that there can be no mistaking the importance of this most Holy Sunday and Holy Week. *The Sunday of the Passion belongs to a comprehensive theology of the cross.* The so-called "triumphal entry" of the Lord into the Holy City is only a part of that story and its theology: the Sunday of the Passion puts this in proper perspective. The problem posed for most preachers is how to reconcile the traditional Palm Sunday theme with the more inclusive theology of the Sunday of the Passion. This may be accomplished through the use of a processional liturgy, which includes a reading of the processional/Palm Sunday Gospel, placing the sermon on the Gospel for the Day in the Liturgy of the Word.

The Prayer of the Day

Most contemporary liturgies provide at least two collects — one for the Palm Sunday processional liturgy and another for the Eucharist. In the very brief LBW "Processional with Palms," for example, there are two prayers. The first is quite compact and, in its very brevity, elucidates the Passion Sunday/Week theme:

> *Mercifully assist us, O Lord God of our salvation, that we may enter with joy upon the contemplation of those mighty acts whereby you have given us life everlasting; through your Son, Jesus Christ our Lord.*

The second prayer concentrates on the triumphal entry into Jerusalem. The first part reads:

> *We praise and thank you, O God, for the great acts of love by which you have redeemed us through your Son, Jesus Christ our Lord. On this day he entered the holy city of Jerusalem in triumph, and was acclaimed the Son of David and King of Kings by those who scattered their garments and branches of palm in his path.*

The second half of the prayer asks for God's blessings upon the palm branches and "those who bear them" in the procession.

Prayers to be used in the liturgy for the Sunday of the Passion are, in the liturgical churches, revisions of the classic collect for Passion/Palm Sunday. This collect precedes the Palm Sunday emphasis and opens up the mystery of the Passion of the Lord. The *Book of Common Prayer* revision goes a bit farther than most:

> *Almighty God, in the tender love for the human race you sent your Son, our Jesus Christ, to take upon him our nature, and to suffer death upon the cross, giving us the example of his great humility: Mercifully grant that we may walk in the way of his suffering, and also share in his resurrection; through Jesus Christ our Lord, who lives and reigns with you and the Holy Spirit, one God, for ever and ever. Amen*

It is clearly, as are the others, oriented toward the Sunday of the Passion as the beginning of Holy Week.

The Psalm of the Day

Psalm 22:1-12, or 22:1-11 (E); 22:7-8, 16-19, 22-23 (R) — The penitential aspects of this psalm make it fit almost perfectly the suffering and death — *and the vindication* — of Jesus. According to St. Matthew, Jesus cried out with the first verse, "My God, my God, why has thou forsaken me?" He probably recited the rest of that verse, if not the entire psalm. When that fact is coupled to the traditional Gospel for the Day (Matthew), it is obvious why this psalm was used on the Passion Sunday early in Christian history. It responds to the first reading and harmonizes with the Gospel for the Day quite handily. It is the perfect psalm for the Sunday of the Passion and the beginning of Holy Week.

The Psalm Prayer (LBW)

> *Father, when your Son was handed over to torture and felt abandoned by you, he cried out from the cross. Then death was destroyed, and life was restored. By his death and resurrection save the poor, lift up the downtrodden, break the chains of the oppressed, that your church may sing your praises; through your Son, Jesus Christ our Lord.*

Psalm 31:1-5, 9-15 (L) — (Note: The LBW appoint this psalm for all three years of the lectionary cycle.) Comments on this psalm may be located in Cycle/Series A.

The readings:

Isaiah 50:4-7 (R); 50:4-9a (C)

The Roman Catholic *Ordo* and the Common and Lutheran lectionaries all assigned this reading to Passion Sunday in Series/Cycle A, as well as in B. Commentary may be found in the *Lectionary Preaching Workbook, Cycle A.*

Isaiah 45:21-25, or 52:13—53:12 (E)

The Episcopal Church stands alone in the selection of these two optional readings for the Sunday of the Passion. There are several reasons why this lection was chosen for the Liturgy of the Word. One of them is the statement attesting to God's uniqueness in verse 21: "And there is no other god besides me, a righteous God and a Saviour; there is none besides me." Verse 23 offers another reason for this choice: "To me every knee shall bow, every tongue shall swear," or as Paul would put it, "every tongue confess that Jesus Christ is Lord to the glory of God the Father." This quotation, of course, is the last verse of the second reading for the day, Philippians 2:11. Verse 25 of Isaiah points to God's victory in Jesus Christ: "In the Lord all the offspring of Israel shall triumph and glory."

Isaiah aptly describes what happened to Christ in his suffering and death, especially in the latter part of the pericope. Verse 3 begins: "He was despised and rejected by men; a man of sorrows, and acquainted with grief; and as one from whom men hide their faces he was despised, and we esteemed him not. Surely he has borne our griefs and carried our sorrows; yet we esteemed him stricken, smited by God, and afflicted. *But he was wounded for our transgressions, he was bruised for our iniquities; upon him was the chastisement that made us whole, and with his stripes we are healed. All we like sheep have gone astray*

. . . and the Lord has laid on him the iniquity of us all . . . .'' It is rather obvious why the Christians incorporated this reading along with Psalm 22 in the early liturgies. It expresses what happened to Jesus — for our sake — very graphically.

Zechariah 9:9-10 (L)

This reading pictures the "king who comes to you; triumphant and victorious is he, humble and riding on an ass, and a colt the foal of an ass." It belongs to the traditional Palm Sunday Gospel of the triumphant entry of Jesus into the Holy City. The opening verses call for rejoicing in the One who has come, while the last part of the reading enunciates the results (the end of war and peace, as a starter) of this new "blood-covenant" which is the great act of restoration on the part of God. This section points to and beyond the suffering and death of Christ to the results that will accrue in the resurrection — the final triumph of God in Jesus Christ.

Philippians 2:5-11 (E, L, C); 2:6-11 (R)

This lection, too, was read last year and commentary made on it in the *Lectionary Preaching Workbook, Cycle A.*

Mark 14:1—15:47, or 14:1-39 (R, L); 14:32-72, 15:1-39 (40-47) (E)

Most congregations will virtually insist that the shorter form of this Gospel be read on the Sunday of the Passion. The longer version is simply too long for the contemporary worshiper to listen to, unless it is cast in the form of a dramatic reading with several voices, one for each character in the reading. Such a production, which could even be done in the form of a chancel drama replete with costumes, might even be attempted. Why, as many congregations do, limit such productions to the mid-week services during Lent? The point is this: *most people will not hear the whole story of the Passion during Holy Week if they do not hear it on Passion Sunday. To participate to the fullest in Good Friday and Easter Worship, people need to rehearse and relearn the Passion story at the end of Lent.*

The shorter reading (15:1-39) highlights the suffering and death of Jesus and puts this event in proper perspective. Although Mark combines two early crucifixion stories — one of which pictures Jesus in terms of Psalm 22 and Isaiah 53 and the other showing a more cosmic context and meaning to the crucifixion of the "King of the Jews" — he is still able to give the whole his own theological interpretation. Reginald Fuller writes:

> *This narrative (the second of the two stories in verses 25, 26, 29a, 32b, 33, 34a, 37, and 38) interprets Jesus' death not as that of an innocent, righteous suffering servant of God but as an agonizing conflict between the powers of light and the powers of darkness. This is an apocalyptic interpretation. The loud cry of Jesus is an announcement of triumph of the power of light (and implicitly Jesus' exaltation), and the rending of the temple veil, a symbolical expression of that victory. We have here an interpretation of the death of Jesus which recalls the hymn in Philippians 2:6-11. Jesus is the divine redeemer who has emptied himself of his divine glory and therefore it is concealed from the powers of darkness who are his enemies. They therefore crucify the lord of glory (1 Corinthians 2:8). His death leads to his exaltation and triumph over the powers.*
>
> *(Preaching the New Lectionary,* p. 352)

Had Mark used only one or the other of these narratives, a defective theology of the cross would have resulted. On one hand, Jesus' death would be that of a good man who lived an exemplary life, and for that was condemned to death and crucified. Such a death would have limited significance for the faith. The second story, without the first, would tend toward abstraction (the "light" and "darkness" theme). Together, they show that the innocent one, who suffered and died at Calvary, came to that end through his perfect obedience to God's will and plan, and in that terrible and agonizing — and totally undeserved death on a cross — Jesus actually triumphed over his enemies and the forces of darkness, sin, and death.

A Sermon on the Gospel, Mark 11:1-10 and 15:1-39 (E, C) — "A Temporary Triumph."

Some years ago, a colleague of mine gave me a copy of an old engraving, which depicted Kaiser Wilhelm's visit to Jerusalem early in this century. When the Kaiser entered the Holy City for the first time, he was mounted on a magnificent white stallion, instead of on a colt like Jesus. Instead of going through one of the gates of the city, he had a new entrance chopped out of the walls to make his entrance unique. He rode through that gap and staged his version of his triumphal entry into the city of Jerusalem. He was, indeed, a conqueror — temporarily — in his own right, but his triumphal entry bore no resemblance to that of Jesus (not anything like the results of Jesus' glorious entrance). The world has forgotten about the Kaiser's triumphal entrance into Jerusalem, partly because he and his army went down to an ignominious defeat in World War I, but the story of Jesus' entrance into Jerusalem will be told forever — along with the full story of what happened in the following week that led to complete victory for God over the forces of darkness and evil.

1. *It was a temporary triumph that Jesus experienced on the day known as Palm Sunday.* He soon ran into opposition, intrigue, betrayal and desertion, a mock trial, suffering and death on the cross. The triumph of Palm Sunday was temporary when it should have been permanent. After all, this entrance was prophesied by Zechariah and represented the redemption in the world.

2. *The triumph of his enemies appeared* to be an ultimate triumph. It seemed to mean an end to Jesus' mission, as well as to his life, here on earth. When the opposition couldn't intimidate Jesus and get him to recant, they sent him packing — to Herod and the cross. The Jews got rid of Jesus forever. That's what they thought. They hated Herod's placard that was nailed with Jesus to the cross — "The King of the Jews." They wanted to have the imposter killed — and he was.

3. *But their triumph was also temporary.* God took a hand in the proceedings and raised up Jesus, as scripture said he would, on the third day. They could kill Jesus, but they could not keep him in the tomb. (See the sermon, "You Can't Nail Jesus Down" in the volume of sermons edited by John Killinger, *Experimental Preaching.*) Jesus' victory at the tomb has eternal significance. Sin and death and evil and darkness were all defeated when Jesus died and came forth from the grave on the third day.

4. *God made Jesus' temporary victory a lasting one* — he has made him King of Kings and Lord of Lords, ruler of heaven and earth. And because he lives, we shall also live forever in his kingdom. Alleluia! Alleluia! Alleluia!

Sermons on the First and Second Lessons

Sermon suggestions for the Isaiah 50 and Philippians 2 readings are included in the commentary for the Sunday of the Passion in the *Lectionary Preaching Workbook, Cycle A.* Rather than preach an entire sermon on the Isaiah 45 or the Isaiah 52-53 text, I would incorporate the main content and, perhaps quotations, in number two of the above sermon.

Maundy Thursday

(Note: The Episcopal Church employs the same three readings for all three series/cycles of the church year. The Lutheran Church uses a different set of lessons for years B and C, two of which [Exodus 24 and Mark 14] are set for Corpus Christi [Year B] of the Roman Catholic Church. Since the John 13 text is considered in the sermon suggestions of the *Lectionary Preaching Workbook, Cycle A*, only the Mark 14 reading will be used for the sermon suggestions for Maundy Thursday, Year B.)

The church year theological clue

In addition to the emphasis of reconciliation between God and his people, a central motif of the Maundy Thursday and any service of Holy Communion, the Gospel for Maundy Thursday (Mark 14:12-26) concentrates the attention of the church on one of the other fruits of the Eucharist, the New Covenant God makes with his people in the bloody sacrifice of Jesus Christ at Calvary.

The Prayer of the Day

The *Lectionary Preaching Workbook, Cycle A,* contains comments on LBW prayers, which typically emphasize "a new commandment," "a wonderful sacrament," and "a memorial of your suffering and death." Most Maundy Thursday prayers tend to concentrate on the institution of the Lord's Supper. None mentions the "new covenant" concept of Mark 14:24.

The Psalm of the Day

Psalm 116 — This psalm received attention in the *Lectionary Preaching Workbook, Cycle A*.

Psalm 78:14-20, 23-25 (E) — Here is a recitation of the ordeals of the people of Israel on their forty-year trek through the wilderness, detailing their doubt that God would be able to feed them. He had brought forth water from a rock, but food was another matter. "They tested God in their hearts, demanding food for their craving. They railed against God and said, 'Can God set a table in the wilderness?' " He did — by sending down manna from heaven every single day of their trek. The typology of the psalm points to the meal which Jesus instituted to complete the new covenant that God made in him with all people.

The readings:

Exodus 24:3-11 (L)

The significance of this passage for Maundy Thursday is that it reveals the role of sacrificial blood in the covenants of God: first in the blood that Moses threw on the altar; and second, on the people as well. In Mark 14:24, Jesus says, "This is *my* blood of the covenant, which is poured out for many." The ultimate sacrifice which people can offer to God is their "blood," their life — the ultimate gift that they can make in response to God's grace and mercy. Jesus made that sacrifice when he died, and his blood was, in a sense, poured up on the altar of God. But that blood must also be "thrown" on the people of God, and that takes place in the Eucharist. William Cowper put it this way in one of his hymns:

> *There is a fountain filled with blood*
> *Drawn from Immanuel's veins;*
> *And sinners, plunged beneath that flood,*
> *Lose all their guilty stains*

> *Dear dying Lamb, thy precious Blood*
> *Shall never lose its power;*
> *'Till all the ransomed Church of God*
> *Be saved, to sin no more.*

The blood of Christ is "put upon" the people of God when they receive the cup he gave.

Exodus 12:1-14a (E)

Part of the Exodus story is told in this passage (and a crucial part of it, at that) because this reading speaks of the institution of the Passover by God. It is God who gives detailed instructions about the sacrifice of a lamb, ordering the Israelites to put some of the blood on the lintel and the doorposts of their homes, and to roast and consume the entire lamb. Anything left over is to be burned the next morning. (This may have been partly responsible for the practice in some Christian denominations of drinking all of the wine, or pouring any not consumed upon the ground, although it doesn't account for "reserving" the leftover bread.) The last verse directs the people to comprehend this "memorial" and to celebrate it as a "feast to the Lord."

1 Corinthians 10:16-17 (18-21) (L)

It is the shorter reading that has relevance to the Mark 12 Gospel, because Paul explains the meaning of the Holy Communion to the congregation at Corinth. In a way, he turns the sacrament around, because he speaks first about the blood, and only then about the bread. The "cup of blessing," as he calls the act of drinking wine, is actually "a participation" in the blood — the death — of Jesus Christ. By receiving the cup, his blood covers the faithful communicants. The bread, in the same manner, is a participation in the body of Christ. Since there is one loaf, there is one body and believers are members of it. The longer reading had literal meaning for the Corinthian Church, but little meaning for Christians today.

1 Corinthians 11:23-26 (27-32) (E)

This text received consideration and commentary in the *Lectionary Preaching Workbook, Cycle A.*

Mark 14:12-26 (L)

Mark makes it clear in this pericope that the Holy Communion is, for him and the early church, a Christian Passover. The Easter vigil, built as it is around the pertinent Old Testament reading, affirms the connection between the Passover of the Jews and the Passover of Christians in the death and resurrection of Jesus Christ. Mark, therefore, simply shows how the Eucharist was celebrated in the church to which he belonged. He gives no details of the Passover meal, which must have preceded the Lord's Supper. Perhaps the practice in Corinth of a common meal that preceded the Holy Communion was a development from the Passover meal, as well as active participation in the body of Christ. Mark merely records part of the formula, "Take; this is my body," but he says of the cup, "This is *my blood of the covenant*, which is poured out for many." Here, then, is the theological connection between the Exodus 24 reading and this lection, for as the blood was thrown upon the people by Moses as participation in the Covenant, so the drinking of the cup (Jesus' "blood") is participation in the New Covenant established in Jesus' death.

John 13:1-5 (E)

The *Lectionary Preaching Workbook, Cycle A,* considers this reading and gives homiletical commentary and sermon suggestions for parish preachers.

A Sermon on the Gospel, Mark 14:12-26 (L) — "From Soothsayer to Savior."

One of the interesting details in this story is that there was an "unknown man of Holy Thursday." (Dr. Harry F. Baughman, for President and Professor of Preaching at the Lutheran Theological Seminary in Gettysburg, once preached a sermon that was titled, "The Unknown Man of Palm Sunday." One could virtually duplicate that sermon for Maundy Thursday, and one could develop an interesting and, even, intriguing homily.) But the spotlight is on Jesus, not on the "unknown man," who owned the home where the "last supper" was held. For the second time in the story, Jesus is cast in the role of a soothsayer, a prophet who, like Elijah and Elisha, was able to foretell certain events that would take place in the future. On both of those occasions (the first was his entrance into Jerusalem), Jesus predicted that the disciples would find an "unknown man," one of whom would be the owner of the colt, the other would be the owner of a home, who obviously knew about Jesus and may even have been one of his followers. This story shows Jesus as something of a soothsayer first, which was preliminary to his role as Savior.

1. *Jesus demonstrated that he had the power of a soothsayer when the time was at hand for his arrest, conviction, and crucifixion.* His prediction about the man carrying a jug of water was correct. The man gave over to Jesus and the disciples an upper room in his home for the Passover meal.

2. *Jesus turned the Passover into a Christian celebration of the goodness and grace of the loving Father for all of the people in the world.* He instituted a new supper, which involved the eating of bread and the drinking of wine — his body and his blood — by the faithful.

3. *The cup, to Mark, is the guarantee that the sacrifice of Christ on the cross means that the blood of Christ has been, as it were, splattered upon every human being.* And just as the blood of the lamb Moses showered on the people in the Exodus account of the Passover, so the blood of Jesus protects and washes clean every person who drinks of that cup — his blood. It is indeed the blood of the New Covenant and it is meant for all people.

4. *So, as we remember his death, we recall his words as we come to his table, "This is my body . . . . This is my blood of the covenant, which is poured out for many."*

(Note: I would not preach a sermon on the Exodus/Passover reading, but would more likely incorporate it, perhaps in the form of a story/illustration, in the sermon on Mark 14. The emphasis on Maundy Thursday is on the meal that belongs to the "new passover" in Jesus' death and resurrection.)

Good Friday

(Note: single set of readings appointed for Good Friday received homiletical consideration in the *Lectionary Preaching Workbook, Cycle A*. A sermon was developed from Matthew 27, rather than one from the appointed Gospel, John 18:1—19:42 or John 19:17-30. A sermon suggestion from the John 18 and 19 Gospel follows for Series/Cycle B.)

The readings:

John 18:1—19:42

John tells the story of Jesus' betrayal, arrest, trial, and crucifixion somewhat differently than do the synoptic writers. In fact, each one of the four evangelists includes different details and tells the story from his own perspective. For example, all four tell about the incident in the garden, when Peter drew a sword and cut off the ear of the high priest's slave — but only Luke writes that Jesus immediately healed the man, and only John says that the slave's name was Malchus, and only Luke reports that Pilate sent Jesus to Herod because he was a citizen in Herod's jurisdiction. Matthew, among the three writers of the synoptics, mentions Caiaphas by name as the high priest. John, too, names Caiaphas, but he alone involves Annas in the proceedings. The four do not agree on what Jesus said on the cross: John and Luke record three sayings of Jesus (six of the seven sayings come from these two evangelists), and Matthew and Mark only report one of Jesus' last words and the same word at that. John is the only one who mentions Annas by name and describes his part in the proceedings. All of the evangelists tell the same story, but they tell it differently. John's version is the most intriguing.

John not only mentions that the first part of the trial takes place before Annas, the father-in-law of Caiaphas, but he also reports the proceedings in detail. Annas, the former high priest, was the one whom Jesus had offended where it hurt — in the pocketbook — because Annas owned the stalls in the temple where the sacrificial victims were sold. He was a religious racketeer, and he had to get back at Jesus. He did so by refusing to release Jesus — interrogating him about his teaching — and breaking the law in the process. Jewish law called for the testimony of witnesses. Jesus urged, "Ask those who have heard me, what I said to them; they know what I said." Obviously condemning Jesus illegally, Annas sent Jesus on to Caiaphas, *but none of the proceedings before Caiaphas was reported.* Caiaphas apparently rubber-stamped Annas' accusation and had Jesus taken to Pilate for another trial and, hopefully, a death sentence. And as everyone knows, Pilate, although he was convinced that Jesus was innocent, condemned him to death by crucifixion. The trial before Pilate is more detailed than the other accounts — and much more intriguing — as though John might be attempting to fix most of the blame for Jesus' execution on Pilate.

Again, John's version of the crucifixion is somewhat different than those of the other three evangelists. He has Jesus carrying his own cross. But he, too, reports that Pilate had a "King of the Jews" placard placed on the cross above Jesus' head. He mentions that the soldiers gambled for Jesus' clothing and, by doing so, fulfilled scripture. The three "words" Jesus spoke are different: 1.) "Woman, behold your son!" and "Behold, your mother;" 2.) "I thirst;" and 3.) "It is finished." He is the only one who mentions that the soldiers had to break the legs of the other two criminals so that they could be buried before the sabbath, and that Jesus was already dead so his legs were not broken, although his side was pierced by a spear. Both of these facts fulfill scripture. John says nothing about the veil of the temple being torn, nor about graves being opened and people rising from the dead when Jesus died. He does conclude the story of the crucifixion of Jesus with the account of Joseph of Arimathea, who went secretly to Pilate and asked for Jesus' body and buried Jesus in a new tomb in a nearby garden before sundown.

From time to time, if not annually, it is desirable to tell the full story of Jesus' crucifixion on Good Friday, simply because most people have forgotten it and/or have neglected to read or thing about it. This sermon suggestion is intended to do just that — tell the story from John's perspective as "A Likely Story."

1. *The arrest in the garden.* Judas was the one who got a group of soldiers together, took them to the garden, and stood there while they questioned and arrested Jesus. He did not, according to John, identify Jesus by kissing him. He not only didn't have the courage to do that, but that would have been too direct, too open, and Judas appears to have been too much of a schemer, as well as a coward, for that.

2. *The contrast.* Jesus boldly asked, "Whom do you seek?" and answered their "Jesus of Nazareth" with, "I am he." He turned himself over, but he also protected his disciples with his "let these men go." They must have done as Jesus requested, because John says nothing about their running away and abandoning him. The last act in the garden was that Jesus disarmed Peter, after he cut off Malchus' ear with a sword.

3. *Annas and Caiaphas.* Annas was a religious racketeer and, as the power behind the throne, the organizer of the inquisition. He was out to get even with Jesus — and he really did, although he had to go through the formality of sending Jesus to Caiaphas, and then on to Pilate.

4. *The missing court record.* Somebody shredded the documents that told about the proceedings before Caiaphas. Did he merely concur — rubber stamp — what had happened before the former high priest? Peter was there and denied — for the third time — that he was a disciple of Jesus. What was in the missing record? All we know is that Caiaphas sent Jesus on to Pilate.

5. *The way of a wimp.* That's what Pilate turned out to be, despite the fact that he was the most powerful man in Jerusalem. He found no fault in Jesus, but simply took the easy way — the way of the wimp — out of the situation. He humiliated and beat Jesus, and then he condemned him to death and released an insurrectionist, Barabbas, to the Jews.

6. *The crucifixion.* Christ carried the cross to Calvary. They nailed him to it and placed a sign above his head: "This is the King of the Jews."

    a. The soldiers divided his clothing and gambled for it.
    b. Jesus spoke to his mother and to John.
    c. Jesus cried out, "I thirst."
    d. He died with a shout, "It is finished."

7. *Burial.* More intrigue — Joseph of Arimathea went secretly to Pilate and asked for Jesus' body in order to bury him before the Sabbath began. Nicodemus joined him and took the embalming spices to the tomb, where — everyone believed — the story of Jesus would come to an end.

8. *It was a likely story.* It all could have happened the way that John relates it. It is so true to life, to the evil that "lurks in the hearts of men" — and women and children, too. John was not afraid to tell this likely story, because he knew how it would all come out. And so do we.

Easter Vigil

(Note: Details about the Easter Vigil are included in the *Lectionary Preaching Workbook, Cycle A*. In addition, it should be said that baptism is the sign and sacrament of the Christian Passover, Jesus' death and resurrection. In this sacrament, people are "sealed by the Holy Spirit" into the body of Christ, the church, and are "marked with the Cross of Christ forever." The importance of emphasizing the renewal of the baptismal covenant as a key element in the Easter celebration is simply that God, once more, renews his new covenant in Christ with the faithful. The God, who has given his Son to die for the world, affirms in the Easter event that he will love his people forever. At the same time, the people of God renew their baptismal vows, resolving that, through the power of the Holy Spirit operating in their lives, they will lead new lives in obedience to Jesus' command, "Be perfect, even as I am perfect." Since the Sacrament of Holy Baptism is followed up by the Holy Meal, at which the living Lord is the Host, the Easter worship is more than the declaration of the resurrection — "He is risen" — and the singing of a few of the lovely Easter hymns, it is the actual participation in the resurrection of Jesus Christ right now through the word and the sacrament of font and table.

A Sermon on Baptism, Mark 10:39b

> *The cup that I drink you will drink; and with the baptism with which I am baptized, you will be baptized . . . .*

In *The Militant Ministry*, Hans Reudi Weber reconstructs what Holy Baptism might have been like on the Island of Rhodes in the early Christian church. The members and candidates gathered about a large cross carved into a flat rock on the top of a mountain just before dawn on Easter. The candidates were placed on the western side of the cross, there to undergo the final part of their examination and exorcism. Just as the sun began to rise, they were led — one by one — down three steps into the water-filled cross and asked the three-fold question, "Do you believe in God, the Father Almighty . . . . and in Jesus Christ, his Son, our Lord, . . . and in the Holy Spirit . . . ?" Three times each person replied, "I believe," and each time (the candidate) was immersed completely — "drowned" — in the water of the cross-font. The newly baptized came up out of the chilly water and climbed out of the cross by way of the steps on the eastern arm — just as the first rays of the sun were announcing the resurrection of Jesus Christ. Confirmation followed and then they joined the congregation in the Easter Eucharist at the Table of the Lord. If Weber is at all accurate in this attempt to show what baptism was like in the early church, it is safe to conclude that those people never forgot their baptism and the meaning of baptism in their lives. No wonder they were willing to live, even die, for their faith in Jesus Christ! (This was taken from a sermon, "Baptism — A Gift of God," in my first book on baptismal preaching, *Plastic Flowers in the Holy Water*. A somewhat similar reconstruction was done by Martin Marty in his book, *Baptism*. He uses the "apostolic traditions" of Hippolytus for his reconstruction.)

1. Jesus' baptism, begun in the Jordan River, was only completed when he died on the cross at Calvary. Early in his ministry, he could say — looking toward the cross — "I have a baptism to be baptized with." Christ our passover is sacrificed for us!

2. Our baptism — like that of Jesus — will not be completed until we die. The resurrection of our Lord reassures us and gives us hope that we, too, will be raised up to everlasting life.

3. Through the renewal of our baptism on Easter, we die through repentance and rise to a new life — a life of love, obedience, daily repentance, renewal, and caring service in the name of the Lord.

4. At the table of othe Lord, we not only "proclaim his death until he comes again," but the living Lord also joins us in this special meal, feeds us, and gives us joy, hope, and peace. We know that in our baptism, God has made an eternal covenant with us and that because he lives, we too shall live forever with him.

The Resurrection of Our Lord

Roman Catholic	Acts 10:34-43	Colossians 3:1-4	John 20:1-9
Episcopal	Acts 10:34-43	Colossians 3:1-4	Mark 16:1-8
	or Isaiah 25:6-9	or Acts 10:34-43	
Lutheran	Isaiah 25:6-9	1 Corinthians 15:19-28	Mark 16:1-8
			or John 20:1-9 (10-18)
Common	Isaiah 25:6-9	1 Corinthians 15:1-11	John 20:1-18

The church year theological clue

In the beginning of the Christian era, there was only the Resurrection of Our Lord. That was the chief — and only — festival that the early church celebrated. The reality of the resurrection caused the worship to be shifted from Friday night and Saturday (the Sabbath) to Sunday because the Lord was raised from the dead on the first day of the week. So once a year, the church celebrated Easter Day, as it is now called, but every Sunday was also a commemoration of the victory of Jesus Christ over the cross and the grave. That's all there was, as far as the liturgical year was concerned — Easter and Sunday, celebrating the death and resurrection of our Lord.

Christians, right from the start, recognized the centrality of the resurrection of Jesus Christ for their faith and life. Without the triumph over the tree and the tomb, they knew — with Paul — that their faith would have been in vain. They would still be bound by their sins, and worst yet they would only remember Jesus as a misguided martyr who had given the world some lovely teachings and a model of sacrificial living that matched his teachings. Few of the early Christians would have allowed themselves to be killed had they not been convinced that Jesus was alive again — forever. The Jewish converts would have reverted to Judaism — or drifted away from their faith altogether — and the Gentiles would have gone back to their old gods and their old ways of worship. Jesus would probably have been remembered as a magician, a teacher, and something of a prophet, but not much more. The impact of Christianity then would have been diminished, and today the Christian faith would mean even less than it does.

The resurrection does not in any way diminish the willing and obedient death of Christ upon the cross; rather it magnifies it by putting it in the perspective of God's plan to redeem the world and reconcile all people to himself. It *was* necessary for Jesus to die so that God could engage in a new act of creation in which he would "make all things new." The death of Jesus makes it impossible for people to celebrate Easter casually. The cross is always on the other side of it, and Easter allows no mere theology of glory that diminishes, or eliminates, the actual pain and suffering that Jesus underwent in his passion and death on Golgotha.

This combination — the death and resurrection of the Lord — was probably what prompted the church to celebrate the Easter victory for fifty days, the Great Fifty Days of the Pasch. In the *Ordo* and the lectionaries of the other liturgical churches, this fifty-day pattern of celebrating the resurrection is re-established, but it has not really "caught on," as yet. Lent remains the "essential season," at least in practice. It is up to the parish preachers to recognize the importance of the Festival of Festivals, and that Easter is a fifty-day observation of Christ's victory over the cross and death, and do something about re-establishing Easter as the Great Fifty Days in the public worship of the church and the lives of the people. Easter is — and needs to be — more than a few "alleluia's" and "Christ is risen!" because *he really rose from the tomb on Easter Day. His resurrection means that we, too, shall live forever with him.*

The Prayer of the Day

The reconstruction of the classic collect for Easter Sunday, the Resurrection of Our Lord, was discussed in the *Lectionary Preaching Workbook III, Cycle A,* but it should be emphasized that it clearly relates to renewal in baptism — not simply on Easter Day, but every day of our lives. The opening note on John 3:16 ("O God, you gave your only Son to suffer death on the cross for our redemption") is followed by what his death accomplished ("and by his glorious resurrection you delivered us from death"), and is completed by this petition: "Make us die every day to sin, so that we may live with him forever in the joy of the resurrection." It is by daily repentance — and the grace of God — that we die to sin and live in the hope of everlasting life (which was, it should be said, one of the favorite sayings of Luther in conjunction with baptism). Baptism is a continuing "death and resurrection" process that is only finished at the end of his life.

The liturgical churches have prepared several other prayers for the principal service and the other services of Easter. The revised classic prayer, however, accommodates all three series/cycles of lectionary readings because it has retained its baptismal orientation to Easter. Easter, again, is the baptismal occasion *par excellence* of the church.

The Psalm of the Day

Psalm 118:1-2, 15-17, 22-23 (R); 118:1-2, 15-24 (L); 118:14-29, or 118:14-17, 22-24 (E) — Here is a psalm that might have been used on many different occasions by the Jews. Some scholars think it was first sung when the walls of Jerusalem were completed during the reign of Nehemiah. But it is particularly well-suited as a psalm that celebrates what God has done in the resurrection of Jesus Christ — and especially what that momentous event means for people: "Give thanks to the Lord, for he is good; his mercy endures forever." The liturgical churches cut it up to accommodate their Easter liturgies. All, however, employ verses 22-24 in the responsory to the first reading: "The same stone which the builders rejected has become the chief corner stone. This is the Lord's doing, and it is marvelous in our eyes. On this day the Lord has acted; we will rejoice and be glad in it." The last verse (29) repeats the opening theme, which is so appropriate to the meaning of the resurrection: "Give thanks to the Lord, for he is good; his mercy endures forever."

The Psalm Prayer (LBW)

Lord God, your Son, rejected by the builders, has become the cornerstone of the church. Shed rays of your glory upon your church, that it may be seen as the gate of salvation open to all nations. Let cries of joy and exultation ring out from its courts to celebrate the wonder of Christ's resurrection, now and forever.

The readings:

Isaiah 25:6-9 (E, L, C)

The eschatological banquet, as Isaiah envisions it, was the first reading in the Roman Catholic *Ordo* for the Twenty-eighth Sunday in Ordinary Time/the Twenty-first Sunday after Pentecost, Cycle/Series A. In addition to the comments in the *Lectionary Preaching Workbook III, Cycle A,* it should be said that this reading (which finds fulfillment in the resurrection of Jesus Christ) is also given an eschatological dimension. There will be a time when "the end" will come and God will bring the history of humanity on earth to the conclusion that he has planned ever since the beginning of time. With the resurrection of Jesus, people begin to participate in that meal ("As often as you eat this bread and drink this cup, you proclaim the Lord's death until he comes again.") of thanksgiving and hope.

Acts 10:34-43 (R, E)

It was pointed out in the *Lectionary Preaching Workbook III, Cycle A,* that the book of Acts replaces readings from the Old Testament during the Easter season. The Roman *Ordo* appoints only one set of lessons for Easter Sunday (Acts 10:34-43, Colossians 3:1-4, and John 20:1-9). The Episcopal *Book of Common Prayer* assigns the Acts 10 reading as the first reading in all three years of the lectionary, but also selects an alternate Old Testament reading for each set of pericopes. Additional commentary is located in the *Lectionary Preaching Workbook III, Cycle A.*

Colossians 3:1-4 (R, E)

With the *Ordo*, the *Book of Common Prayer* lectionary assigns Colossians 3:1-4 as the second reading for all three cycles/series of the church year. In the BCP lectionary, the Acts 10:34-43 reading is an alternate lesson. Commentary on Colossians 3:1-4 has been included in the *Lectionary Preaching Workbook III, Cycle A.*

1 Corinthians 15:1-11 (C); 15:19-28 (L)

The Lutheran and Common lectionaries both choose the 15th chapter of 1 Corinthians, Paul's great chapter on the centrality of the death ("for our sins") and resurrection of Jesus for Christian faith and hope, but they use different parts of it. In this reading, Paul also lists the appearances of the risen Lord — to Cephas/Peter, to the twelve, to 500 people, to James and all of the apostles, and "last of all as to one untimely born, he appeared to me" (an apparition which Paul did not deserve, because he persecuted the church of God). It is this Gospel of God's love, power, and mercy in Jesus Christ that Paul had preached to the Corinthian congregation when he had visited Corinth a few years earlier. He reminds them of this to correct the theological deficiencies and spiritual "back-sliding" that had occurred in their community. In the process, he reminds his readers in every age about the nature and content of the Good News in Jesus Christ.

The Lutheran lectionary begins with Paul's famous assertion, "If in this life only we have hope in Christ, we are of all men most to be pitied." His argument is simply that because Christ has been raised up from the dead, those who believe in him and know that their sins are forgiven will also be raised up to eternal life. Jesus is the "first-fruits" of that resurrection, the one through whom the longed-for hope of overcoming death in the Old Testament has finally become a reality. In time, the "last enemy" — death — will be overcome, and "all things will be put under his feet." It is then that Christ will claim his final victory, already begun by his resurrection. Christians may surely believe that Gospel and base their hope in the risen Lord.

John 20:1-9 (R); 20:1-18 (C, L)

The Common and Lutheran lectionaries (the Lutheran lectionary appoints Mark 16:1-8 as the Gospel for the Day, with John 20:1-18 as an alternate reading) repeat the first part of Mary Magdalene's experience on that first Easter morning and conclude with Jesus' appearance to her in the garden of the resurrection (verses 11-20). Peter and "the other disciple," who had run to the tomb after Mary Magdalene had reported that the grave had been opened, "went back to their homes" not knowing what to think or believe. Mary stayed and, in her grief, looked into the tomb and saw two angels, who engaged her in conversation about her weeping. Before the angels could answer her "because they have taken my Lord away, and I don't know where they have laid him," she turned around and was asked the same question that the angels had asked, "Woman, why are you weeping?", by a man she assumed to be the gardener. When he called her by name, "Mary," she recognized him. He told her not to hold on to him, but to go and tell his disciples that she had seen him. She found them and said, "I have seen the Lord." Interestingly, John does not mention their reaction to Mary's testimony.

Mark 16:1-8 (E, L)

These eight verses of scripture reveal all that Mark knew about the resurrection of Jesus Christ. First, he knew that Mary Magdalene and two other women went to the tomb to complete the burial procedures early on Sunday morning wondering how they would get into the tomb. The tomb had been opened — the stone had been rolled away — and Christ was gone. Second, they entered the open tomb and encountered an angel, who nearly scared them to death. He reassured them that Jesus had risen from the dead — "He has risen, he is not here; see the place where they laid him." Third, the angel gave them an order, which pointed to Jesus' post-resurrection appearances, "But go, tell his disciples and Peter that he is going before you to Galilee; there you will see him, as he told you." Fourth, the women fled in near panic and, according to Mark, said nothing to anyone about their experience. History (the open tomb), tradition (the resurrection), and reaction (the "appearances" in Galilee) are clearly perceived in this short Gospel. Homiletically, the last verse pulls it all together for people today.

A Sermon on the Gospel, John 20:1-9 (R, L) — "The Great Resurrection Day Race."

1. *A death march by Mary Magdalene preceded the resurrection race.* Her march to the tomb ended in a surprise — the tomb had been opened — and she ran the first lap of the race to tell Peter and John (?) what she had seen.

2. *Peter and "the other disciple" raced one another to get to the tomb first. Peter lost the race, but he was the first to enter the empty tomb.* "The other disciple" also went in and saw what Peter saw — the cloths and the napkin — and the Gospel says that "he believed." John says nothing about Peter believing what the evidence suggested, adding, "for as yet they did not know the scripture, that he must rise from the dead."

3. *They walked back to their homes.* Why verse 10 is not part of this Gospel is puzzling, but it needs to be incorporated into this sermon. This is where we come in, because we know that they should have run back into the city — into the world — with the Good News about the resurrection. Instead, they went home and *waited* for something more to happen. Are we, who have heard the story of Jesus' resurrection, really much different than Peter and the other disciple?

4. *It is up to us to continue the resurrection race* by going into the world and shouting as loudly as we can, particularly by the quality of our lives, "Christ is risen! He is risen indeed! Alleluia!" It is up to us, because we have been incorporated into Jesus' death and resurrection in our baptism, which the word and sacraments renew today.

A Second Sermon on the Gospel

(Note: Those who might be preaching on the more inclusive Gospel might use a similar approach to the one above, but would incorporate the first appearance to Mary Magdalene in it. The sermon might look like this and have this title — "Run, Mary! Run!")

1. *Mary ran to tell Peter and "the other disciple" when she discovered that the tomb had been opened.* Was it good news or bad news that she gave them? What was going on in that garden?

2. *Mary's running became a race between Peter and John (?) to get to the tomb first and find out what had happened.* John won the race, but Peter first saw the evidence of the resurrection. But they didn't understand it, and so they walked back home to wait for further developments.

4. *Mary stayed and when she looked into the tomb, two angels appeared.* (Where were they when Peter and John went into the tomb?) They asked, "Woman, why are you weeping?" Suddenly, Jesus was there and she recognized him after he called her by name, "Mary." She called him "Teacher." We may — and should — call him "Teacher and the Risen Lord." We celebrate the resurrection with Mary today.

4. *Mary obeyed Jesus.* He told her to go and report what she had seen and experienced to Peter and the other disciples. She became the first Christian evangelist. She was the first person, according to the Gospel of John, to tell the Good News to others. Genuine celebration of the resurrection of Jesus has to have that dimension to it. The news is too good to keep to ourselves. Mary would have told the disciples without any orders from Jesus because the news was too good to keep to herself. What does the Gospel mean to us?

A Third Sermon on the Gospel, Mark 16:1-8 (E, L) — "The Tale That Was Not Told."

1. *An unpleasant task* (the embalming) and a serious problem (the removal of the stone from the tomb) were resolved for Mary Magdalene and the other woman. The stone was rolled away and the tomb was open. What now?

2. *A frightful encounter* took place. An angel was there and spoke to them. He told them not to be amazed and that Jesus, whom they sought, was risen from the dead. That was too much to believe; they had seen him die on the cross.

3. *They might have been scared out of their wits,* but they stayed when they could have run — and so they heard that the Risen Lord would appear to Peter and the disciples. That should have been Good News to them. Was it?

4. *They kept all of this to themselves.* They were afraid to say anything. Was it the angel's appearance? Didn't they believe him? Or if they did believe, was it that they feared that they might not be believed that the news was too incredible? Did they fear the authorities, who would soon hear about the empty tomb? Or what? At least they had good reason for not telling the Good News, but what about us?

5. *The tale was not told right away* — but it has been told and believed ever since.

A Sermon on the First Lesson, Isaiah 25:6-9 (C, L, E)

A sermon suggestion for this reading is included in the comments for the Twenty-first Sunday after Pentecost (which is also Proper 23 in the Common and Episcopal lectionaries) and the Twenty-eighth Sunday in Ordinary Time (Roman Catholic *Ordo*). It is appropriate, with a few rather obvious adjustment for Easter Sunday.

A Sermon on the Second Lesson, Acts 10:34-43 (R, E) and Colossians 3:1-4 (R, E)

Sermon suggestions for these two texts can be located in the *Lectionary Preaching Workbook III, Cycle A.*

A Sermon on the Second Lesson, 1 Corinthians 15:1-11 (C) — "This is the Good News."

1. It tells of the death and resurrection of Jesus, according to Paul.

2. The resurrection of Jesus was confirmed by his appearances to the disciples, apostles, and others, including the Apostle Paul.

3. That's what we have to base our belief in the Risen Lord on. But it is more than enough, because we have been incorporated into that death and resurrection through our baptism.

4. We believe that Jesus died and rose on this day, so we celebrate his resurrection with joy and thanksgiving.

1 Corinthians 15:19-28 (L) — "Death Will Be Destroyed."

1. The resurrection means that death will finally be destroyed.

2. Jesus is our ultimate hope; we shall be made alive — forever — in him.

3. God will finally restore things so that all will be as he intended it to be.

4. We shall live with him forever.